EASY
KETO
DINNERS

flavorful low-carb meals for any night of the week

Carolyn Ketchum

VICTORY BELT PUBLISHING
Las Vegas

First Published in 2018 by Victory Belt Publishing Inc.

ISBN-13: 978-1-628602-77-7

The author is not a licensed practitioner, physician, or medical professional and offers no medical diagnoses, treatments, suggestions, or counseling. The information presented herein has not been evaluated by the U.S. Food and Drug Administration, and it is not intended to diagnose, treat, cure, or prevent any disease. Full medical clearance from a licensed physician should be obtained before beginning or modifying any diet, exercise, or lifestyle program, and physicians should be informed of all nutritional changes.

The author/owner claims no responsibility to any person or entity for any liability, loss, or damage caused or alleged to be caused directly or indirectly as a result of the use, application, or interpretation of the information presented herein.

Front and back cover photos by Hayley Mason and Bill Staley

Interior design by Yordan Terziev and Boryana Yordanova

Printed in Canada

TC 0218

CONTENTS

PREFACE

Committing to the keto lifestyle is hard enough sometimes. Why make it harder with complicated dinner recipes that require difficult-to-find ingredients?

You have better things to do than to spend all your time in the kitchen prepping low-carb, high-fat meals. This cookbook is all about making your life easier so you can enjoy everything the ketogenic diet has to offer without becoming a slave to your stove. Here you will find dinner recipes that put a premium on simplicity—minimal prep time and straightforward cooking techniques that bring out the best flavors, all without wasting your precious time.

I have to tell you that *Easy Keto Dinners* was an absolute joy to write. Because I too need help cutting down on time in the kitchen. I too have those moments of looking around at the end of the day, wondering how time slipped away from me. Or those days when I really don't want to think about dinner at all. And with a hungry, growing family, those can be moments of pure panic. What the heck am I going to feed these ravenous people? Why do they demand dinner every single day? How quickly can I get a solid, healthy meal on the table that will please every palate?

As followers of this wonderful keto way of life, we don't have the luxury of relying on convenient prepackaged meals. That's a good thing, of course, for both our bodies and our minds. But while intricate, multistep recipes can be fun sometimes, they don't fit in well with our busy day-to-day lives. Having reliable and easy keto recipes at our fingertips is a key factor in sticking with, and loving, this low-carb, high-fat lifestyle.

What's the number-one reason people succumb to temptation and fall off the wagon? A lack of delicious and healthy keto meals ready when they need them. Been there, done that. Haven't we all? The aim of this cookbook is to give you more weapons in your dinnertime arsenal so that you never have to feel deprived.

Healthy eating has never been so easy . . . or so delicious!

INTRODUCTION:

EASY
DOES IT!

Before we jump into the recipes, let's define what constitutes an easy recipe.

"Easy" doesn't always mean fast. While quick recipes are always useful, they might actually require more hands-on work than a slow-cooked meal that has virtually no prep time. Sometimes it's about getting things into your oven or slow cooker quickly so you can enjoy some downtime. I am a huge fan of slower recipes that practically cook themselves. That way, I have more time to help my kids with their homework or get them to soccer practice. Or, you know, actually talk to my husband once in a while. Now there's a novel idea.

This cookbook contains both easy-quick and easy-slow keto dinner recipes. We can all use some of both, depending on the day, the time, and the circumstances. If you plan ahead, popping some ingredients into your slow cooker early in the day enables you to come home to a fully cooked meal. But on those crazy days when life gets away from you, it's wonderful to have recipes that come together in thirty minutes or less. And on a lazy Sunday afternoon, it's ideal to pop an easy roast or stew into the oven and let its aroma fill the house while you enjoy some time with friends or family.

Also, don't be intimidated by longer ingredient lists. Often, many of those ingredients are just spices and seasonings that intensify the flavor of your dish. Adding them is simple.

The goal of all these recipes is to keep effort and prep time to a minimum while maximizing flavor. That's what *Easy Keto Dinners* is all about.

EASY TIPS AND SHORTCUTS

Oh, where on earth do I start? I have so many tips and tricks that will make your life easier and your dinner prep simpler. Remember, I've been doing this for seven long years, so I've become a deft hand at keto dinnertime. As much as I love to cook, saving time and energy in the kitchen is paramount to me. Three hungry kids with a myriad of after-school activities leave me short on time most weeknights. Don't even get me started on soccer season!

Plan Ahead

Planning ahead is without question the biggest time-saving tactic. We all know we should do it, but busy schedules mean that sometimes we don't. Sometimes even our best-laid plans get away from us—unless you happen to be one of those ultra-organized people who always has everything under control (in which case, I'm sorry, but we can't be friends). I am not one of those ultra-organized people and I never will be. So I will skip the lecture on the virtues of meal planning except to say that it's a great idea if you can manage it.

If you can't plan ahead or if your plans go awry, don't panic. There are plenty of shortcuts that can help you get a healthy keto dinner on the table.

Don't Reinvent the Wheel

Most keto cookbooks suggest that you should make everything from scratch. Bone broth! Cauliflower rice! Mayonnaise! Seasoning blends! Don't get me wrong, I love making these things at home. But if I did it all from scratch, I would never have any time for cooking anything else. Not to mention how much freezer and fridge space these things can take up.

So I am giving you permission, right here and right now, to use the store-bought versions of some staple ingredients. As long as you choose wisely, neither your recipes nor your health will suffer. And the good news is that with the increasing popularity of low-carb and Paleo diets, many brands are getting in on the action. There are so many healthy keto options, you never have to feel guilty about not making them yourself.

It is, however, important to be a label reader. Check those carb counts and look for sources of added sugar and starch. Here are a few items I recommend keeping on hand:

- Bone broth—Pacific Foods and Kettle & Fire have great-tasting bone broths in easy-to-use cartons.

- Jarred tomato sauce—Look for brands with no added sugars that have no more than about 4 grams of carbs per ½ cup. I like Rao's Homemade.

- Mayonnaise—I like avocado oil–based mayo from Primal Kitchen or Chosen Foods.

- Salsa and other sauces—Frontera has some good low-carb choices, as does La Victoria.

- Seasoning mixes—Many seasoning brands add fillers and starches to prevent clumping, but Primal Palate and Spiceology are two brands that I trust. I also enjoy ordering bulk spices from Penzey's. Be sure to read the ingredient lists, as some of the rubs contain sugar.

Check out the "Recommended Convenience Foods" section on pages 156 to 158 for more of my favorite ready-made foods.

Let Someone Else Do the Prep Work

These days, all grocery stores carry bags of precut and prewashed vegetables for your convenience. While they may lose a little bit of nutrition compared to fresh whole veggies, they can make your life considerably easier. Think about it: in a time crunch, the choice may be between preprepped veggies or no veggies at all. Which option do you think is healthier?

There are so many choices, from bagged salads to broccoli florets to prechopped onions and celery. And with the rising popularity of cauliflower rice and zucchini noodles, some grocery chains now carry these as well. While I tend to buy most vegetables in their whole form, I have been known to take advantage of these convenient options from time to time.

Do look for packages that contain the freshest-looking veggies, and make sure they aren't past their best-by date. Plan on consuming them within a day or two of purchase, because cut vegetables spoil faster than whole ones. Sturdier vegetables like broccoli and cauliflower hold up better than more fragile peppers and zucchini.

Let Someone Else Do the Cooking

No, I am not suggesting that you get someone else to make the whole meal. That would be what we call "takeout." However, using precooked meats in some easy dinner recipes cuts down significantly on the overall cooking time. Most grocery stores have hot rotisserie chickens available for purchase, which can be an easy keto meal in itself. The leftovers can then be utilized in soups, salads, and casseroles for a second easy meal. (You'll find a few ideas on the next page.) See, I just solved two nights' worth of dinners for you!

Fully cooked sausages are another great option. Most kielbasa and smoked sausage comes fully cooked, so you don't have to take the time to cook it through before adding it to a recipe. My husband recently discovered a grass-fed beef sausage at Costco called Teton Waters Ranch. It's our go-to smoked sausage now. There are also several brands of chicken sausage that come fully cooked, like Al Fresco and Aidells. Precooked vacuum-packed sausage can last up to several months in the fridge, so you don't have to remember to thaw it ahead of time.

However, do read the labels carefully. Many sausages contain junky fillers and preservatives. Also keep in mind that some varieties, even from trusted brands, contain added sugars or maple syrup for flavor. I stick with the brands that don't add preservatives, and I choose the varieties that have 1 gram of carbs or less per serving.

5 easy ideas for rotisserie chicken:

Chicken Enchilada Skillet (page 22)

Southwestern Chicken– Stuffed Avocados (page 30)

Buffalo Chicken Chowder (page 34)

Thai Chicken Salad (page 40)

Chicken Parmesan Casserole (page 42)

Frozen Is Fabulous . . . and Sometimes Healthier

Frozen vegetables are incredibly useful for quick meals, and sometimes they don't even need to be thawed. If they do require thawing, soaking them in some warm water and then draining them can speed up the process. Better yet, frozen veggies are incredibly nutritious, as they are flash-frozen at the peak of freshness to lock in nutrients. They do lose something in terms of texture and consistency, so they aren't appropriate for every recipe, but I always have frozen broccoli, spinach, and artichoke hearts in my freezer. And the frozen riced cauliflower that many stores now carry is a mainstay of my healthy cooking.

One of my all-time favorite shortcuts is to use frozen garlic and herbs. I think I can safely say that the little frozen crushed garlic cubes from Dorot have saved me hours of mincing and chopping time. Dorot also makes crushed basil, cilantro, and ginger. They are like little flavor bombs for easy keto meals. Again, they do lose a little in the freezing process (I find the garlic more mellow than fresh garlic, for example), but they are so great in a pinch. And they are available in the freezer section at many grocery stores.

Thaw Foods Quickly

Forgot to take some protein out of the freezer to thaw? Don't panic. And believe me when I say that I've been there . . . more times than I care to admit.

You don't have to wait hours for your chicken, fish, or beef to defrost in the fridge. Quick thawing methods like setting the frozen protein in a bowl of cold water work very well, and your protein can be ready to go in twenty to thirty minutes. Some sources I consulted say that warm water is fine and doesn't cause bacteria to grow because there isn't time, so it depends on what you are most comfortable with. I usually use the cold-water method. Here are a few tips:

- Make sure that the meat is well sealed in a resealable plastic bag. You don't want the meat to come in direct contact with water, as this can change how it cooks. The only exception to this rule is frozen shrimp. You can simply put the shrimp in a colander or sieve and run cool water over it until thawed. Make sure to pat the shrimp dry before cooking.
- Weight the package down with something heavy so that it stays submerged.
- If the package contains several pieces of meat, pull them apart as soon as they are defrosted enough. They will thaw more quickly this way.
- If your recipe requires thinly sliced meat, slice it while it's still semi-frozen. This helps a great deal in getting thin, even slices for recipes like stir-fries.
- Cold-water thawing is best for smaller items like steaks, chicken thighs, and pork chops. Larger pieces of meat really do need to thaw for a day in the fridge.

You can actually cook some proteins, like boneless chicken breasts and fish fillets, from frozen. But unless your recipe calls for it, I don't recommend it as a general rule. Frozen foods release moisture as they thaw, and that can change the water content of the dish.

That being said, I do sometimes add "mostly thawed" ground beef or pork to a pan and continue to break up the meat as it cooks. This saves me five minutes or so on the thawing time.

Soften Up

Does a recipe require softened butter or cream cheese? No worries. Simply place the butter or cream cheese in a microwave-safe bowl and zap it on high in fifteen-second increments. Press gently with your finger to test the softness. If the bottom part of the butter or cream cheese begins to liquefy, stop there.

Chop It Up

Ingredients that are cut into bite-sized chunks always cook faster than larger pieces. This is particularly true for meats that need to be cooked through. Although it can mean a little more prep work, chopping cuts down significantly on your cooking time. So if you're in a huge hurry to get dinner on the table, think easy stir-fries or sautés.

Want a really fun, easy tip for chopping fresh herbs? I learned this from a professional chef at a conference, and I could have kissed him, I was so delighted with it. Put your herbs at the bottom of a narrow drinking glass and use scissors or kitchen shears to snip them as you turn the glass. Because the glass keeps them contained, you can get them quite finely chopped in a matter of moments.

Have the Right Tools

Far be it from me to tell you that you have to outfit your kitchen with all the best cutlery and cookware. But the tools you use really can make a difference in how much energy you need to expend making dinner. Sharp knives cut through meats and veggies more easily and safely, and good-quality pots and pans cook food more evenly. A decent food processor or blender can save time on chopping, mashing, and pureeing.

A number of recipes in this book call for a slow cooker, an Instant Pot or other pressure cooker, or a Dutch oven. These cooking vessels are incredibly useful, but you certainly don't need to own all three. I'd say the most important one is a good heavy Dutch oven, as any slow cooker or pressure cooker recipe can be modified for stovetop or oven braising. And a Dutch oven is fabulous for making double or even triple batches of your favorite soups and stews. An Instant Pot certainly does save you time over a slow cooker, but it's not required for making the recipes in this book; I've provided instructions for making all Instant Pot recipes in a slow cooker as well.

An oven thermometer—the kind that stays in your oven—is another worthwhile investment. Even the best ovens tend to run a little hotter or cooler than the temperature setting, and knowing the true temperature of your oven can save you time. You can always set the oven temperature a bit higher or lower than a recipe calls for to get a more accurate cooking time.

Reuse and Recycle

I love leftovers, and I'm not afraid to admit it. We love leftovers in this house so much that we typically double or even triple a recipe calls so that we can stretch it into more than one meal. When you think about it, leftovers really are the smartest way to make your dinners easy, cutting down on effort, time, and expense—not to mention saving landfill space.

For many recipes, you can simply reheat and eat the leftovers the same way you made the dish the first time. But it's fun to get creative and use them in entirely new ways, too. Here are some of my favorite ways to repurpose leftovers:

- **Frittata or omelet**—Leftover meats and vegetables can be chopped up and used in an egg dish. And frittatas are so easy to make. Check out the Bacon, Mushroom & Swiss Frittata on page 90.

- **Salad**—Leftover chicken, steak, or fish makes a great hearty salad. Try the Thai Chicken Salad on page 40.

- **Soup**—I sometimes make "kitchen sink soup" with whatever leftovers I have on hand. I just sauté some onions in a bit of oil, then add some broth and bring it to a simmer. Then I add leftover meat and/or veggies and heat until warmed through.

- **Stir-fry or sauté**—Simply chop up the leftovers, then heat up some oil in a skillet and stir-fry or sauté until warmed through. Because they are already cooked, the meal will come together in a matter of moments.

Finally, many dishes can be frozen after cooking. Try to choose things that won't get soggy or change in consistency too much in the freezing process. And consider portioning them out into individual servings for quick lunches or dinners when you're on your own.

STOCKING YOUR
EASY KETO KITCHEN

Obviously, having all the ingredients you need on hand for a given recipe is going to make life considerably easier. But once again, that's the ideal scenario, and real life rarely lives up to such ideals. Still, there are a few things I try never to run out of, because then I know I can always pull something together on the fly.

5 THINGS YOU SHOULD ALWAYS HAVE IN YOUR FREEZER:

SHRIMP
Peeled and deveined.

FROZEN VEGETABLES
A bag of spinach and a bag of broccoli, and frozen riced cauliflower if you can find it.

BACON
It's practically a keto law that you must always have bacon on hand.

CHICKEN
Boneless, skinless thighs work perfectly for quick keto dinners.

GROUND BEEF
Stock up when you see a sale!

---

5 easy ideas for ground beef:

Bacon Sloppy Joes
(page 66)

Jalapeño Cheddar Stuffed Burgers
(page 74)

Mexican Cauliflower Rice Skillet
(page 76)

Instant Pot Meatloaf
(page 78)

Cincinnati Chili
(page 82)

---

5 THINGS YOU SHOULD ALWAYS HAVE IN YOUR PANTRY:

CANNED COCONUT MILK — Great for soups and curries.

CHICKEN BROTH — Homemade or not, this ingredient is mandatory.

CANNED TUNA — Healthy and easy.

Cheater's Tomato Sauce (page 137) saves the day!

TOMATO PASTE

COCONUT OIL — Ideal for quick stir-fries.

5 THINGS YOU SHOULD ALWAYS HAVE IN YOUR FRIDGE:

FRESH LOW-CARB VEGGIES — Bell peppers, broccoli, cauliflower, lettuce, zucchini . . . have at least one or two of these.

CREAM CHEESE — Useful for making creamy soups.

MAYONNAISE — Tuna melts for the win!

EGGS — If you have eggs, you've always got something for dinner.

Flavor and fat in one delicious package.

BUTTER

HOW TO USE
THIS BOOK

Easy Keto Dinners contains fifty main-course recipes and ten "extras"—delicious side dishes and a few condiments to round out your meals. I wrote this cookbook with the average family in mind, so most of the recipes make four to six servings. But many of them can easily be scaled up or down according to your needs. I've tried to stay away from specialty ingredients, so you should be able to find almost everything at your local grocery store.

Nutritional Information

The chapters are organized by the main protein, and every recipe includes key nutritional information per serving: calories, fat, protein, total carbohydrates, and fiber. All the nutritional information was calculated using MacGourmet, a software program that relies on the USDA National Nutrient Database. I strive to be as accurate as possible, but these numbers are often only estimates based on the average size of certain ingredients. I encourage you to calculate your own nutritional information whenever possible.

Quick Reference Icons

I've included some fun icons to show you just how each recipe will make your life easier. Need dinner in a jiffy? Want to prep something ahead for the next day? Planning to use your slow cooker? Yep, I've got a recipe (and an icon!) for that.

 FAMILY-FRIENDLY—Nothing is more disheartening than making a meal for unappreciative children. Trust me, I am all too familiar with this feeling. So if a recipe gets the family-friendly rating, it means that all three of my kids liked it. GASP!

FREEZER-FRIENDLY—Trying to get a jump on your meal planning? Smart! This category includes recipes that can be frozen after being cooked, as well as a few that can be prepped and frozen uncooked.

MAKE-AHEAD MEAL—While all the meals in this book can be eaten right after they are made, some taste even better the next day. And a few can be prepped ahead of time and cooked later.

30 MINUTES OR LESS—From start to finish, including prep time, these are the recipes to turn to when you're in a hurry, because they come together in half an hour or less.

ONE-PAN WONDER—These recipes use a single pan so you have less work to do after dinner.

SIMPLY SLOW-COOKED—Slow-cooked recipes equal maximum flavor. This category includes recipes that are made in a slow cooker as well as those that cook slowly in the oven.

Allergens

Being mindful that many people suffer from food allergies or intolerances, I have noted which recipes contain major allergens. About 50 percent of the recipes are dairy-free or can be made dairy-free, and those recipes are designated with a dairy-free icon. I've offered dairy-free substitutions where possible. The vast majority of the recipes in this book are egg-free or nut-free or both. Recipes that *do* contain those ingredients are designated by egg and/or nut icons.

Well, now that you know how to use *Easy Keto Dinners*, what are you waiting for? Let's get cooking!

CHAPTER 1:

CHICKEN

CHICKEN ENCHILADA SKILLET

Who needs tortillas with their chicken enchiladas? The fillings and sauce are the best part anyway, and this skillet dinner is so much easier to make. But if you're dying for a wrap to go with it, check out the Pork Rind Wraps on page 142.

Yield: 6 servings   Prep time: 5 minutes   Cook time: 25 minutes

2 tablespoons salted butter

1½ pounds boneless, skinless chicken breasts, cut into large chunks (about 4 inches each)

Salt and pepper

1 cup chicken broth

2 tablespoons tomato paste

1 tablespoon chili powder

½ teaspoon garlic powder

½ teaspoon ground cumin

⅛ teaspoon cayenne pepper

¾ cup sour cream

1½ cups shredded cheddar cheese or Mexican cheese blend (about 6 ounces)

1. In a large skillet over medium heat, melt the butter. Season the chicken generously with salt and pepper. Brown the chicken in the butter for about 2 minutes per side.

2. Add the broth and bring to a simmer. Cook for 12 to 15 minutes, until the chicken is cooked through.

3. Remove the chicken to a plate and remove about half of the broth from the skillet. Discard the broth. Whisk the tomato paste, chili powder, garlic powder, cumin, and cayenne into the remaining broth in the skillet. Shred the chicken with 2 forks.

4. Reduce the heat to low and whisk in the sour cream until well combined. Stir in the chicken. Sprinkle the cheese over the top and cover the skillet until melted, about 4 minutes.

SERVING SUGGESTION: *Serve with cauliflower rice and your favorite enchilada toppings, like pickled jalapeños, cilantro, guacamole, and tomatoes.*

MAKE IT EVEN FASTER! *Use cooked rotisserie chicken instead of fresh chicken breasts. Just be sure to reduce the amount of broth to ½ cup so your sauce isn't too saucy. Add the broth along with the tomato paste and spices.*

NUTRITIONAL INFORMATION   CALORIES: 351 | FAT: 19g | PROTEIN: 34g | CARBS: 3.2g | FIBER: 0.7g

CILANTRO LIME GRILLED CHICKEN

This is a fantastic recipe for meal planning. You can either make it right away or freeze it uncooked for future use. And you aren't limited to this single marinade, either. Think lemon garlic, curry, or taco-spiced chicken thighs.

Yield: 4 servings **Prep time:** 5 minutes (not including time to marinate)
Cook time: 20 minutes

MARINADE:

¼ cup fresh lime juice

¼ cup chopped fresh cilantro

2 tablespoons avocado oil

2 cloves garlic, minced

2 teaspoons grated lime zest

1 teaspoon salt

½ teaspoon black pepper

½ teaspoon ground cumin

½ teaspoon red pepper flakes

1¼ pounds boneless, skinless chicken thighs

1. In a gallon-size resealable plastic bag, combine the ingredients for the marinade. Add the chicken thighs and massage the bag with your hands to coat the chicken in the marinade.

2. Press out as much air as possible and seal the bag tightly. Let marinate in the refrigerator for at least 1 hour or up to overnight.

3. Preheat the grill to medium. Remove the chicken from the bag and discard the marinade. Grill the chicken until nicely browned and cooked through, 8 to 10 minutes per side. The internal temperature should reach 165°F on an instant-read thermometer.

Freezer Instructions for Uncooked Chicken: Complete Steps 1 and 2, then place the sealed bag in the freezer for up to 1 month. Let thaw completely before cooking.

SERVING SUGGESTION: *My family likes this chicken paired with a simple salad or some cauliflower rice and lime wedges. It's also really great as part of the salad itself.*

NUTRITIONAL INFORMATION CALORIES: 211 | FAT: 12g | PROTEIN: 28.1g | CARBS: 2.2g | FIBER: 0.3g

ITALIAN CHICKEN & VEGGIE FOIL PACKETS

Foil packet dinners are ideal for minimal cleanup. You can serve them right out of the packet—no need to dirty any dinner plates! This is a great way to pair chicken with fresh vegetables from your garden.

OPTION

Yield: 4 servings   Prep time: 15 minutes   Cook time: 25 minutes

1¼ pounds boneless, skinless chicken thighs, cut into 1-inch chunks

1 medium zucchini, sliced ¼ inch thick

1 medium-sized red bell pepper, sliced

1 cup chopped green beans

1 medium tomato, cut into large chunks

¼ cup thinly sliced onions

2 ounces sliced mushrooms

1 clove garlic, minced

¼ cup avocado oil

1 tablespoon chopped fresh rosemary

1½ teaspoons salt

1 teaspoon dried oregano leaves

½ teaspoon black pepper

Grated Parmesan cheese, for serving (optional)

1. Preheat the oven to 400°F. Cut 4 pieces of aluminum foil, each about 12 inches square.

2. In a large bowl, combine the chicken, zucchini, bell pepper, green beans, tomato, onions, mushrooms, and garlic. Drizzle with the oil, then sprinkle with the rosemary, salt, oregano, and pepper. Toss to combine well.

3. Divide the mixture evenly among the pieces of foil, arranging it down the center of each piece. Bring up the two sides of the foil and fold over together twice to seal. Fold up the ends tightly.

4. Place the packets on a rimmed baking sheet and bake for 25 minutes, or until the chicken is cooked through.

5. Remove the packets and open the top seams. Sprinkle with grated Parmesan cheese, if using. Eat directly from the packets or transfer to plates.

 *Simply leave off the Parmesan cheese.*

NUTRITIONAL INFORMATION   CALORIES: 280 | FAT: 19.4g | PROTEIN: 30.2g | CARBS: 9.4g | FIBER: 3.1g

ONE-PAN JAMAICAN JERK CHICKEN & "RICE"

I love jerk chicken, but Scotch Bonnet peppers aren't easy to come by. This dry seasoning emulates the same flavors and is not overly spicy, so even younger palates can enjoy it. Feel free to amp up the heat if you prefer.

Yield: 4 servings   Prep time: 5 minutes   Cook time: 36 minutes

JERK SEASONING:

1½ teaspoons granular erythritol

1 teaspoon salt

¾ teaspoon ground allspice

½ teaspoon black pepper

½ teaspoon cayenne pepper

½ teaspoon garlic powder

½ teaspoon paprika

½ teaspoon dried parsley

¼ teaspoon dried thyme leaves

¼ teaspoon ground cinnamon

¼ teaspoon ground nutmeg

4 bone-in, skin-on chicken thighs

2 tablespoons avocado oil, for the pan

¼ cup chopped onions

12 ounces riced cauliflower

Lime wedges, for serving

1. Preheat the oven to 375°F.

2. In a small bowl, whisk together the ingredients for the jerk seasoning. Rub the seasoning blend all over the chicken.

3. In a large skillet over medium heat, heat the oil until shimmering. Place the chicken skin side down in the pan and cook without disturbing for 4 minutes, until the skin is golden brown. Flip the chicken and cook for another 4 minutes.

4. Remove the chicken to a plate and add the onions to the skillet. Sauté until translucent, about 4 minutes. Add the riced cauliflower and cook until just tender, another 4 minutes.

5. Return the chicken to the skillet, skin side up, and transfer the skillet to the oven. Bake for 20 minutes, or until the chicken reaches an internal temperature of 165°F. Serve with lime wedges.

NUTRITIONAL INFORMATION CALORIES: 487 | FAT: 36.1g | PROTEIN: 33.8g | CARBS: 6.6g | FIBER: 2.3g

SOUTHWESTERN CHICKEN– STUFFED AVOCADOS

Stuffed avocados are the perfect low-carb convenience food.

 (30) Yield: 4 servings   Prep time: 10 minutes   Cook time: —

---

2 medium avocados

2 tablespoons fresh lime juice, divided

Salt and pepper

2 cups chopped rotisserie chicken

¼ cup mayonnaise

1 tablespoon chopped fresh cilantro

¼ teaspoon chipotle powder

½ cup diced tomatoes

2 tablespoons shredded cheddar cheese (optional)

1. Cut the avocados in half and remove the pits. Use a spoon to scoop out some of the flesh, leaving a ½-inch-thick wall inside the skin. Reserve the avocado flesh for another use. Brush each avocado half with lime juice and sprinkle lightly with salt and pepper.

2. In a medium bowl, mix together the chicken, mayonnaise, remaining lime juice, cilantro, and chipotle powder until well combined. Season with salt and pepper to taste. Gently fold in the diced tomatoes.

3. Divide the chicken salad among the avocado halves and sprinkle with the cheddar cheese, if desired.

 **DAIRY-FREE OPTION** *Simply leave off the shredded cheese.*

NUTRITIONAL INFORMATION   CALORIES: 356 | FAT: 29.2g | PROTEIN: 15.6g | CARBS: 7.5g | FIBER: 4.9g

CHICKEN COCONUT CURRY

Every time I eat curry, I wonder why I don't have it more often. The cooking process is simple, and the end result is flavorful and comforting. Note to self: make more curries! This dish is fantastic served over cauliflower rice.

 Yield: 4 servings Prep time: 10 minutes Cook time: 25 minutes

¼ cup coconut oil

1 small zucchini, sliced ¼ inch thick

¼ cup chopped onions

2 tablespoons curry powder

½ jalapeño pepper, minced

1½ pounds boneless, skinless chicken thighs, cut into ½-inch pieces

Salt and pepper

1 cup full-fat coconut milk

½ cup chopped fresh tomatoes

¼ teaspoon xanthan gum (optional)

3 tablespoons chopped fresh cilantro, for garnish

1. In a large skillet over medium-high heat, heat the coconut oil until shimmering. Add the zucchini and onions and sauté until the onions are translucent, about 4 minutes.

2. Stir in the curry powder and jalapeño and cook until fragrant, another 30 seconds. Sprinkle the chicken with salt and pepper and place in the skillet. Sauté until nicely browned all over, about 5 minutes.

3. Add the coconut milk and bring to a simmer. Reduce the heat to medium-low and cook for 10 minutes, until the chicken is fully cooked through. Stir in the tomatoes.

4. For a thicker sauce, push the chicken and veggies to the side of the skillet and sprinkle the sauce with the xanthan gum. Whisk quickly to combine, then toss with the rest of the curry.

5. Sprinkle with chopped cilantro before serving.

NUTRITIONAL INFORMATION CALORIES: 461 | FAT: 31.8g | PROTEIN: 35.7g | CARBS: 6.2g | FIBER: 2.5g

BUFFALO CHICKEN CHOWDER

My son loves Buffalo sauce so much; we go through it at an alarming rate. I practically had to wrestle the bottle away from him so that I could use some to create this recipe!

(30) Yield: 6 servings   Prep time: 10 minutes   Cook time: 15 minutes

2 tablespoons salted butter

2 stalks celery, chopped

½ cup chopped onions

¾ teaspoon salt

½ teaspoon black pepper

1 tablespoon tomato paste

3 cups chicken broth

¼ cup Buffalo-style wing sauce

4 ounces cream cheese (½ cup), softened

1 cup heavy whipping cream

3 cups chopped rotisserie chicken

Chopped celery, for garnish

Crumbled bleu cheese, for garnish

1. In a large saucepan over medium heat, heat the butter until frothy. Add the celery and onions and sauté until the vegetables are tender, about 4 minutes. Season with the salt and pepper.

2. Whisk in the tomato paste until well combined, then add the broth and Buffalo sauce. Bring to a boil, then reduce the heat to a simmer.

3. Place the cream cheese in a blender or food processor and add about 1 cup of the hot broth. Blend until smooth, then add the cream cheese mixture to the saucepan.

4. Stir in the cream and bring back to just a simmer, then stir in the chopped chicken and heat briefly to warm through. Divide the soup among 6 bowls and garnish with chopped celery and bleu cheese.

NUTRITIONAL INFORMATION CALORIES: 376 | FAT: 29.6g | PROTEIN: 18.2g | CARBS: 4g | FIBER: 0.5g

BACON SPINACH FETA CHICKEN

👪 (30) ⏲ Yield: 6 servings   Prep time: 10 minutes   Cook time: 20 minutes

6 slices bacon, chopped

6 boneless, skinless chicken thighs

Salt and pepper

1 tablespoon salted butter

2 cloves garlic, minced

5 ounces baby spinach

1 cup heavy whipping cream

½ ounce Parmesan cheese, grated (about ½ cup)

¾ cup crumbled feta cheese (about 3 ounces)

1. In a large skillet over medium heat, cook the bacon until crisp, about 5 minutes. Remove to a paper towel–lined plate to drain, leaving the bacon grease in the pan.

2. Season the chicken thighs with salt and pepper and place in the skillet, laying them flat. Cook for 4 minutes per side or until cooked through. Remove to a plate.

3. Add the butter to the skillet. When melted, add the garlic and cook for 1 minute, until fragrant. Add the spinach and sauté until wilted, 2 to 3 minutes.

4. Stir in the heavy cream and Parmesan and cook until thickened, about 3 minutes. Add the bacon to the sauce and stir to combine. Return the chicken to the skillet and toss to coat. Sprinkle the crumbled feta over the top.

SERVING SUGGESTION: *Serve over zucchini noodles or cauliflower rice.*

NUTRITIONAL INFORMATION   CALORIES: 423 | FAT: 27.9g | PROTEIN: 34g | CARBS: 3.3g | FIBER: 0.5g

SLOW COOKER WHITE CHICKEN CHILI

This dairy-free chicken chili gets its creaminess from the addition of frozen cauliflower. If you have a large enough slow cooker, consider making a double batch and freezing the leftovers. This recipe can also be made in an Instant Pot or other pressure cooker.

 Yield: 4 servings   Prep time: 10 minutes   Cook time: 4 hours

---

1½ pounds boneless, skinless chicken thighs

3 cups chicken broth

12 ounces frozen cauliflower florets

1 (4.5-ounce) can mild green chilies

¼ cup bacon grease or coconut oil

¼ cup chopped onions

1 jalapeño pepper, minced (leave the seeds in for more heat)

2 cloves garlic, minced

2 teaspoons ground cumin

1 teaspoon salt

¼ teaspoon black pepper

Chopped fresh cilantro, for garnish

1. Put all of the ingredients except the cilantro in a 4- to 6-quart slow cooker. Cook on high for 4 hours or on low for 8 hours.

2. Remove the chicken to a plate and shred with 2 forks. Use an immersion blender to blend the soup until it is mostly creamy. Return the chicken to the slow cooker and mix well.

3. Divide among 4 soup bowls and sprinkle with cilantro.

SERVING SUGGESTION: *This is the sort of soup that benefits from lots of delicious toppings. If you don't need to be dairy-free, then sour cream and shredded cheese are delicious. Chopped avocados, jalapeño slices, and a lime wedge give it great flavor as well.*

INSTANT POT METHOD: *Cook on the soup/stew function for 35 minutes. Allow for a natural pressure release.*

NUTRITIONAL INFORMATION   CALORIES: 373 | FAT: 18.6g | PROTEIN: 37.9g | CARBS: 9g | FIBER: 3.1g

THAI CHICKEN SALAD

A hearty salad can, and indeed *should,* be the main meal sometimes. This salad marries my love of peanut chicken with crunchy cabbage for a distinctively Asian twist.

(30) Yield: 4 servings   Prep time: 10 minutes   Cook time: —

DRESSING:

3 tablespoons peanut butter

2 tablespoons avocado oil

2 tablespoons water

1 tablespoon apple cider vinegar

2 teaspoons fish sauce

1 clove garlic, coarsely chopped

½ teaspoon ginger powder

¼ teaspoon red pepper flakes

SALAD:

4 cups chopped cabbage

4 cups chopped rotisserie chicken

1 red bell pepper, thinly sliced

1 green onion, white and light green parts only, thinly sliced

2 tablespoons salted peanuts, chopped

2 tablespoons chopped fresh cilantro

1. To make the dressing, combine the dressing ingredients in a blender and blend until smooth. Thin with additional water as necessary.

2. In a large bowl or serving dish, layer the cabbage, chicken, bell pepper, and green onion. Sprinkle with the chopped peanuts and cilantro.

3. Serve the salad with the dressing on the side.

MAKE IT EVEN FASTER! *Grab a bag of prechopped slaw mix instead of chopping your own cabbage. Just be sure it doesn't contain a lot of carrots or other high-carb veggies.*

SUBSTITUTIONS *If you prefer, you can use almond butter in place of peanut butter in the dressing and sliced almonds in place of peanuts on the salad.*

NUTRITIONAL INFORMATION   CALORIES: 310 | FAT: 24.3g | PROTEIN: 23.8g | CARBS: 8.7g | FIBER: 3g

CHICKEN PARMESAN CASSEROLE

This easy Chicken Parm is a huge hit with my whole family. The crushed pork rinds on top act as the "breading." It can be frozen either before baking or after, and it's easy to prep a day ahead. Just be sure to wrap it up tightly with foil before putting it in the freezer or fridge.

 **Yield:** 6 servings   **Prep time:** 5 minutes (not including time to cook chicken)
Cook time: 25 minutes

5 cups cubed cooked chicken

1 cup Cheater's Tomato Sauce (page 137)

½ teaspoon red pepper flakes

1 ounce Parmesan cheese, grated (about 1 cup)

1½ cups shredded mozzarella cheese (about 6 ounces)

1 ounce pork rinds, crushed

½ teaspoon crushed dried basil

1. Preheat the oven to 350°F and lightly grease an 8-inch square baking pan.

2. Spread the chicken in the greased dish and pour the tomato sauce over it. Sprinkle with the red pepper flakes. Top with the Parmesan and then the mozzarella. Lightly sprinkle the crushed pork rinds and basil over the top.

3. Bake for 25 minutes, until the cheese is melted and bubbly.

Variation: Pizza Chicken Casserole. Skip the pork rinds and top with some sliced pepperoni for a fun keto pizza casserole.

MAKE IT EVEN FASTER! *Use your favorite no-sugar-added marinara in place of the easy Cheater's Tomato Sauce.*

NUTRITIONAL INFORMATION   CALORIES: 438 | FAT: 25.6g | PROTEIN: 43.8g | CARBS: 4.2g | FIBER: 0.8g

SPICY TANDOORI CHICKEN

There is something about marinating chicken in yogurt that results in incredibly tender chicken, even when it's subjected to very high heat. Tandoori seasoning gives the chicken a fantastic flavor, making this meal a surprise hit with kids.

Yield: 6 servings   **Prep time:** 5 minutes (not including time to marinate)
Cook time: 35 minutes

MARINADE:

½ cup plain whole-milk yogurt

2 tablespoons tandoori seasoning

2 tablespoons avocado oil

2 tablespoons lemon juice

½ teaspoon cayenne pepper

2½ pounds bone-in, skin-on chicken pieces (thighs and drumsticks)

Salt and pepper

TIP: *Tandoori seasoning is available from many spice companies. I purchased mine from Penzey's, and it contains only ground spices.*

1. In a gallon-size resealable plastic bag, combine the ingredients for the marinade. Add the chicken pieces and massage the bag with your hands to coat the chicken in the marinade.

2. Press out as much air as possible and seal the bag tightly. Let marinate in the refrigerator for at least 3 hours or up to overnight.

3. Preheat the oven to 425°F and arrange the chicken in a single layer on a broiler pan. Drizzle any remaining marinade over the chicken and sprinkle with salt and pepper. Bake for 25 to 30 minutes, until the internal temperature of the chicken reaches 165°F.

4. Turn on the broiler and broil the chicken about 6 inches from the heat for 2 to 4 minutes, watching carefully so it doesn't burn.

Freezer Instructions for Uncooked Meat: Complete Steps 1 and 2, then place the sealed bag in the freezer for up to 1 month. Let thaw completely before cooking.

SERVING SUGGESTION: *Serve with chopped fresh cilantro and lime wedges.*

NUTRITIONAL INFORMATION   CALORIES: 393 | FAT: 27.1g | PROTEIN: 32.5g | CARBS: 2.8g | FIBER: 0.6g

CHAPTER 2:

FISH AND SEAFOOD

GREEK SHRIMP

One of our favorite meals used to be an easy Greek shrimp and rice dish from *Bon Appétit* magazine. With this light and fresh keto version in my repertoire, I don't miss that old high-carb recipe.

(30) Yield: 4 servings   Prep time: 5 minutes   Cook time: 20 minutes

---

3 tablespoons salted butter

2 cloves garlic, minced

1 cup canned diced tomatoes, undrained

¾ teaspoon salt

¾ teaspoon black pepper

½ teaspoon red pepper flakes

1½ pounds medium shrimp, peeled and deveined

½ ounce Parmesan cheese, grated (about ½ cup)

1 cup crumbled feta cheese (about 4 ounces), divided

Chopped fresh parsley, for garnish

1. Preheat the oven to 375°F.

2. In a large ovenproof sauté pan, heat the butter until it begins to froth. Add the garlic and sauté for 30 seconds. Stir in the tomatoes, salt, black pepper, and red pepper flakes and bring just to a simmer.

3. Lay the shrimp in a single layer over the tomatoes, then sprinkle with the Parmesan and ½ cup of the feta. Place the pan in the oven and bake until the shrimp is pink and cooked through, 10 to 15 minutes.

4. Sprinkle with the remaining feta and some chopped fresh parsley before serving.

SERVING SUGGESTION: *Serve over cauliflower rice or buttered zucchini noodles.*

NUTRITIONAL INFORMATION   CALORIES: 287 | FAT: 17.3g | PROTEIN: 22.8g | CARBS: 6.5g | FIBER: 0.7g

BUTTER-ROASTED SALMON WITH LEMONY DILL AIOLI

Fresh salmon is the ultimate quick dinner, as it takes very little time to cook. And a good piece of salmon needs almost nothing but salt, pepper, and maybe a little sauce to accent its flavor.

OPTION

Yield: 4 servings   Prep time: 5 minutes   Cook time: 12 minutes

SALMON:

2 tablespoons salted butter

1 (1-pound) salmon fillet

½ teaspoon garlic powder

Salt and pepper

LEMONY DILL AIOLI:

⅓ cup mayonnaise

1½ tablespoons chopped fresh dill

1 tablespoon fresh lemon juice

2 cloves garlic, minced

TIP: *This is what I call "cheaters' aioli." Instead of spending the time making real aioli from scratch, I whip up a flavorful mayonnaise-based dip.*

1. Preheat the oven to 425°F.

2. Place the butter in a baking pan large enough to hold the salmon. Cut the salmon fillet in half if needed to make it fit. Place the pan in the oven as it's preheating to melt the butter.

3. When the butter is melted, remove the pan from the oven and place the salmon skin side down in the pan. Brush the salmon with some of the melted butter and sprinkle with the garlic powder. Season lightly with salt and pepper.

4. Roast for 9 to 12 minutes, until the fish is opaque and flakes easily with a fork.

5. While the salmon is roasting, make the aioli: In a medium bowl, whisk together the mayonnaise, dill, lemon juice, and garlic. Serve each portion of salmon with a dollop of aioli on top.

 DAIRY-FREE OPTION *Feel free to use coconut oil or avocado oil instead of butter in this recipe.*

NUTRITIONAL INFORMATION   CALORIES: 403 | FAT: 28.7g | PROTEIN: 23.2g | CARBS: 1.1g | FIBER: 0.1g

CALIFORNIA ROLL IN A BOWL

I love sushi, but I've come to realize it's the wasabi and fresh fish that I really love. This sushi bowl enables me to enjoy those flavors and still be grain-free.

OPTION

 30   Yield: 4 servings   Prep time: 15 minutes   Cook time: 10 minutes

WASABI CREAM:

3 tablespoons mayonnaise

1 tablespoon water

2 teaspoons wasabi paste

SUSHI BOWLS:

16 ounces riced cauliflower (about 4 cups), fresh or frozen

2 tablespoons water

1 tablespoon coconut oil

1 tablespoon toasted sesame oil

8 ounces lump crabmeat (canned is fine)

2 tablespoons mayonnaise

2 teaspoons Sriracha sauce

½ avocado, thinly sliced

1 sheet nori, cut into thin strips

½ medium cucumber, cut into matchsticks

Sesame seeds, for garnish

1. To make the wasabi cream, mix the ingredients for the cream in a small bowl until well combined.

2. In a medium saucepan over medium heat, combine the cauliflower with the water and coconut oil. Bring to a simmer, then cover and reduce the heat to low. Cook for 5 to 10 minutes, until tender. Remove from the heat and let cool completely. Stir in the sesame oil.

3. In a medium bowl, combine the crabmeat, mayonnaise, and Sriracha. Stir until well mixed.

4. Divide the cauliflower rice among 4 serving bowls. Top each with one-quarter of the crab mixture, avocado slices, nori strips, and cucumber. Sprinkle with sesame seeds. Serve with the wasabi cream on the side.

NUTRITIONAL INFORMATION   CALORIES: 296 | FAT: 23.6g | PROTEIN: 12.8g | CARBS: 8.6g | FIBER: 3.6g

CLASSIC TUNA MELTS

Tuna salad is the ultimate last-minute dinner recipe. It's healthy and my kids love it, so I know I can rely on it whenever I need a break from cooking.

(30) Yield: 4 servings   Prep time: 5 minutes   Cook time: 2 minutes

2 (5-ounce) cans tuna, drained

¼ cup mayonnaise

1 stalk celery, finely chopped

½ teaspoon lemon pepper

2 batches Coconut Flour 90-Second Bread (page 138)

2 teaspoons salted butter, softened

2 ounces thinly sliced cheddar cheese

1. In a medium bowl, combine the tuna, mayonnaise, celery, and lemon pepper. Use a fork to break up the tuna and mix the ingredients well.

2. Slice the two 90-Second Breads in half and toast lightly. Butter each half and divide the tuna salad between them. Top each with cheddar cheese.

3. Preheat the broiler. Place the tuna melts on a broiler pan and broil 4 to 5 inches from the heat for 1 to 2 minutes, until the cheese is melted. You can also bake tuna melts at 350°F for 5 minutes to melt the cheese. Serve hot.

NUTRITIONAL INFORMATION   CALORIES: 338 | FAT: 26.2g | PROTEIN: 17.8g | CARBS: 3.6g | FIBER: 2g

SMOKED SALMON CHOWDER

This rich, hearty soup tastes just like my favorite appetizer, and it takes just minutes to put together.

(30) Yield: 6 servings   Prep time: 5 minutes   Cook time: 15 minutes

2 tablespoons salted butter

¼ cup chopped onions

1 stalk celery, chopped

½ teaspoon salt

1 clove garlic, minced

1½ cups chicken broth

1 tablespoon tomato paste

4 ounces cream cheese (½ cup)

1½ cups heavy whipping cream

8 ounces smoked salmon (hot smoked), chopped

2 tablespoons capers

2 tablespoons chopped red onions, for garnish

1. In a large saucepan over medium heat, melt the butter. Add the onions and celery and sprinkle with the salt. Sauté until the vegetables are tender, about 5 minutes.

2. Add the garlic and cook until fragrant, another minute. Stir in the broth and tomato paste and bring to a simmer, whisking to combine.

3. Place the cream cheese in a blender and add the hot broth mixture. Blend until smooth. Return the mixture to the saucepan and add the cream, salmon, and capers. Bring back to a simmer over medium-low heat to warm through.

4. Sprinkle each serving of chowder with chopped red onions.

NUTRITIONAL INFORMATION CALORIES: 373 | FAT: 31.4g | PROTEIN: 12.9g | CARBS: 4.6g | FIBER: 0.5g

CREAMY PESTO SHRIMP & ZOODLES

Fresh homemade pesto is lovely, but store-bought pesto can be pretty tasty, too, and it saves you some legwork. Look for brands that are made with olive oil instead of canola oil and have 2 grams of carbs or less per serving.

 Yield: 4 servings   Prep time: 5 minutes   Cook time: 12 minutes

---

2 tablespoons unsalted butter

1 pound large shrimp, peeled and deveined, tails on or off

Salt and pepper

½ cup pesto

½ cup heavy whipping cream

2 medium zucchini, cut into noodles with a spiral slicer

1. In a large skillet over medium-high heat, melt the butter. Once melted, add the shrimp in a single layer and sprinkle with salt and pepper. Let cook undisturbed for 2 minutes, then sauté until cooked through and pink, 1 to 2 more minutes.

2. Remove the shrimp to a plate using a slotted spoon, then reduce the heat to medium. Add the pesto and cream to the skillet and whisk to combine. Bring just to a simmer.

3. Add the zucchini noodles and cook until the desired tenderness is reached, about 4 minutes for al dente. Return the shrimp to the skillet and toss to warm through. Serve immediately.

 *If you don't have a spiral slicer, you can't be part of the keto diet club. I'm kidding, of course, but a spiral slicer really is a helpful tool and is quite inexpensive. It makes living the low-carb life a lot more fun.*

MAKE IT EVEN FASTER! *Many grocery stores sell presliced zucchini noodles in the produce section.*

NUTRITIONAL INFORMATION   CALORIES: 365 | FAT: 27.3g | PROTEIN: 18.8g | CARBS: 7.9g | FIBER: 1.5g

BLACKENED SHRIMP SPINACH SALAD

Flavorful sautéed shrimp takes a dinner salad to the next level. And you will want to drink the creamy avocado dressing!

(30) Yield: 4 servings   Prep time: 10 minutes   Cook time: 5 minutes

AVOCADO RANCH DRESSING:

½ ripe avocado

¼ cup sour cream

¼ cup water

1 tablespoon lime juice

1 clove garlic, coarsely chopped

½ teaspoon dried dill weed

½ teaspoon salt

½ teaspoon black pepper

SALAD:

1½ teaspoons paprika

1 teaspoon garlic powder

1 teaspoon dried oregano leaves

½ teaspoon dried thyme leaves

½ teaspoon black pepper

¼ teaspoon cayenne pepper

1½ pounds medium shrimp, peeled and deveined

2 tablespoons unsalted butter

¾ teaspoon salt

20 ounces baby spinach

¼ medium-sized red onion, thinly sliced into rings

1. To make the dressing, combine the dressing ingredients in a blender and blend until smooth. Add more water to thin it as desired.

2. In a large bowl, combine the paprika, garlic powder, oregano, thyme, black pepper, and cayenne. Add the shrimp to the blackening seasoning and toss well to coat.

3. In a large skillet over medium-high heat, melt the butter. Once melted, add the shrimp in a single layer. Let cook for 2 minutes, then flip the shrimp over and cook for another minute or two, until no longer pink. Sprinkle with the salt.

4. Divide the spinach among 4 salad plates and top each plate with a few onion slices. Divide the shrimp among the plates.

5. Serve with the dressing drizzled over the salads or on the side.

SERVING SUGGESTION: *This salad is also delicious with some shredded cheddar cheese sprinkled on top.*

MAKE IT EVEN FASTER! *You can use store-bought blackening spice or even Cajun seasoning in place of the seasonings listed in Step 2. Many of them have MSG or sugar, so check the labels. Chef Paul Prudhomme has a blackening spice that contains no additives or sugar.*

NUTRITIONAL INFORMATION CALORIES: 275 | FAT: 14g | PROTEIN: 26.4g | CARBS: 8.9g | FIBER: 3.6g

CHAPTER 3:

BEEF

FRENCH ONION POT ROAST

This year, we bought a quarter cow from a friend's farm. There are plenty of chuck roasts, so this recipe is quickly becoming a family favorite. It's perfect paired with riced or mashed cauliflower.

   Yield: 8 servings   Prep time: 5 minutes   Cook time: 8 hours

1 beef chuck roast (about 3 pounds)

Salt and pepper

1 tablespoon avocado oil

1 large onion, thinly sliced

1 cup beef broth

1 tablespoon apple cider vinegar

½ teaspoon onion powder

½ teaspoon dried thyme leaves

1 bay leaf

2 tablespoons salted butter, cut into 2 pieces

1. Season the roast all over with salt and pepper. In a large skillet over medium heat, heat the oil until shimmering. Add the roast and brown on both sides, 5 to 8 minutes.

2. Place half of the sliced onion in a 4- to 6-quart slow cooker. Add the broth, vinegar, onion powder, thyme, and bay leaf. Place the roast on top and arrange the remaining onion slices over the roast. Place the butter on top of the roast.

3. Cook on low for 6 to 8 hours, until the meat is tender. Remove the roast and cut into thick slices. Discard the bay leaf.

4. Serve the roast with the onions and juices. Store leftovers in a covered container in the refrigerator for up to 3 days.

NUTRITIONAL INFORMATION   CALORIES: 457 | FAT: 35.2g | PROTEIN: 32.9g | CARBS: 2.1g | FIBER: 0.4g

BACON SLOPPY JOES

This slightly sweet Sloppy Joe filling gets a flavor boost from crispy bacon bits. Serve it between the low-carb bread option of your choice (see below). You can easily make this dish ahead of time and freeze it as well.

 Yield: 4 servings   Prep time: 5 minutes   Cook time: 25 minutes

4 slices bacon, chopped

1 pound ground beef

½ cup Cheater's Keto Ketchup (page 136)

2 tablespoons powdered erythritol

1 tablespoon Worcestershire sauce

1 tablespoon prepared yellow mustard

1½ teaspoons chili powder

½ teaspoon onion powder

1 clove garlic, minced

1. In a large skillet over medium heat, cook the bacon until crisp, about 5 minutes. Transfer to a paper towel–lined plate with a slotted spoon, leaving the bacon grease in the pan.

2. Add the ground beef to the skillet and cook, breaking up the chunks with a wooden spoon, until almost cooked through but still a little pink, 7 to 10 minutes.

3. Stir in the ketchup, sweetener, Worcestershire sauce, mustard, chili powder, onion powder, and garlic. Reduce the heat to low and simmer for another 10 minutes. Stir the bacon back into the skillet before serving.

SERVING SUGGESTION: *Serve between slices of Coconut Flour 90-Second Bread (page 138) or split Cheesy Drop Biscuits (page 140) with some of my Spicy Refrigerator Pickles (page 134). It's also delicious in a bowl with some shredded cheese on top.*

MAKE IT EVEN FASTER! *If you can find a good sugar-free ketchup, feel free to use it. A lot of them contain sucralose, but Nature's Hollow brand is made with xylitol.*

NUTRITIONAL INFORMATION   CALORIES: 372 | FAT: 23.4g | PROTEIN: 34.5g | CARBS: 4.1g | FIBER: 1.2g

REUBEN SKILLET

Reubens are my favorite! I love all that sauerkraut piled high on thinly sliced corned beef and topped with tangy dressing and melted Swiss. The toasted caraway seeds give this skillet a hint of rye flavor . . . without the bread.

30   Yield: 6 servings   Prep time: 10 minutes   Cook time: 10 minutes

---

RUSSIAN DRESSING:

½ cup mayonnaise

2 tablespoons finely diced dill pickles (page 134)

1 tablespoon tomato paste

2 teaspoons powdered erythritol

¼ teaspoon ground cumin

⅛ teaspoon ground cloves

REUBEN SKILLET:

2 tablespoons salted butter

½ teaspoon caraway seeds

2 cups sauerkraut, drained

12 ounces sliced corned beef, coarsely chopped

8 ounces sliced Swiss cheese

1. To make the dressing, whisk the dressing ingredients together in a medium bowl until well combined. Set aside.

2. In a 10-inch skillet over medium heat, melt the butter. Once melted, add the caraway seeds and toast for about 30 seconds.

3. Add the sauerkraut and sauté to warm through. Spread evenly over the bottom of the skillet. Reduce the heat to medium-low.

4. Top the sauerkraut with the corned beef and drizzle with the Russian dressing. Arrange the slices of Swiss cheese to cover everything. Cover the skillet and cook for 5 minutes, until the cheese is melted.

SERVING SUGGESTION: *Serve on its own or over Coconut Flour 90-Second Bread (page 138). But this deli-inspired meal definitely deserves some homemade pickles (page 134)!*

NUTRITIONAL INFORMATION CALORIES: 468 | FAT: 37.5g | PROTEIN: 21.1g | CARBS: 5.1g | FIBER: 1.6g

BEEF & MUSHROOM STEW

Stew is the perfect lazy Sunday meal. Like many soups and stews, this one gets better as it sits and the flavors meld. Feel free to make it a day or two ahead and reheat it.

Yield: 6 servings   Prep time: 10 minutes   Cook time: 1 hour 45 minutes

2 pounds stew meat, cut into 1½-inch chunks

Salt and pepper

¼ cup bacon grease, avocado oil, or coconut oil

12 ounces cremini or button mushrooms, quartered

¼ large onion, diced

2 cloves garlic, minced

½ cup red wine

1½ cups beef broth

2 sprigs fresh rosemary

1 bay leaf

½ teaspoon xanthan gum (optional)

1. Preheat the oven to 300°F and set an oven rack in the lower middle position.

2. Pat the stew meat dry with paper towels and season generously with salt and pepper.

3. In a Dutch oven over medium-high heat, heat the bacon grease until shimmering. Place the stew meat in the pot and brown, stirring frequently, for 5 minutes.

4. Transfer the beef to a plate and add the mushrooms, onion, and garlic to the pot. Sauté until softened, about 5 minutes. Add the red wine and cook until the wine has reduced by half, another 3 minutes.

5. Stir in the broth, rosemary, bay leaf, browned beef, and any accumulated juices. Bring to a simmer, cover, and transfer the pot to the oven. Cook for 90 minutes, or until the beef is tender.

6. Remove from the oven and discard the rosemary sprigs and bay leaf. Season with salt and pepper to taste. For a thicker gravy, push the meat and mushrooms to one side of the pot and sprinkle the sauce with the xanthan gum. Whisk briskly to combine, then stir into the rest of the stew.

NUTRITIONAL INFORMATION   CALORIES: 483 | FAT: 35.6g | PROTEIN: 30.8g | CARBS: 4.9g | FIBER: 0.8g

GRILLED FLANK STEAK WITH COWBOY BUTTER

Grilling may be the ultimate way to cook a quick and easy meal. Take your grilled steak to the next level with this luscious buttery dipping sauce. The sauce is also great with grilled chicken or fish.

(30) Yield: 4 servings Prep time: 10 minutes Cook time: 10 minutes

STEAK:

1 teaspoon coarse salt

1 teaspoon chipotle powder, or 2 teaspoons chili powder

½ teaspoon garlic powder

½ teaspoon paprika

½ teaspoon black pepper

¼ teaspoon ground cumin

1 tablespoon avocado oil

1½ pounds flank steak

COWBOY BUTTER:

6 tablespoons salted butter, melted

1 tablespoon fresh lemon juice

1 tablespoon chopped fresh parsley or cilantro

2 teaspoons Dijon mustard

1 clove garlic, minced

½ teaspoon salt

¼ teaspoon paprika

⅛ teaspoon red pepper flakes

TIP: *Flank steak can be a tough cut of meat, so it's important to slice it thinly when you are ready to serve it. Always slice against the grain, cutting perpendicular to the muscle fibers.*

1. Preheat the grill to medium-high. In a small bowl, whisk together the salt, chipotle powder, garlic powder, paprika, pepper, and cumin.

2. Brush the oil over both sides of the steak and sprinkle generously with the seasoning mix.

3. Grill the steak for 3 to 5 minutes per side, until the internal temperature reaches at least 135°F on an instant-read thermometer. This will give you medium-rare steak; grill longer if you prefer your steak medium or well-done. Let the steak rest while you make the butter.

4. To make the Cowboy Butter, whisk together the ingredients in a medium bowl.

5. Slice the steak thinly against the grain and serve with the Cowboy Butter for dipping.

NUTRITIONAL INFORMATION CALORIES: 440 | FAT: 30.3g | PROTEIN: 36.7g | CARBS: 1.8g | FIBER: 0.7g

JALAPEÑO CHEDDAR STUFFED BURGERS

Stuffed burgers pack a fabulous flavor punch and really don't take much more effort than basic burgers. With that gooey center spilling out, you don't even need a bun. This is a job for a knife and fork!

 Yield: 4 burgers   Prep time: 20 minutes   Cook time: 12 minutes

2 ounces cream cheese (¼ cup), softened

½ cup shredded cheddar cheese (about 2 ounces)

1 large jalapeño pepper, seeded and minced (leave the seeds in if you prefer more heat)

1 pound ground beef

1½ teaspoons salt

1 teaspoon black pepper

½ teaspoon ground cumin

½ teaspoon garlic powder

1. In a medium bowl, combine the cream cheese, cheddar cheese, and jalapeño. Use a fork to mash together well.

2. In a large bowl, combine the ground beef, salt, pepper, cumin, and garlic powder. Use your hands to mix the ingredients well.

3. Divide the beef mixture into 4 even portions. Take about two-thirds of a portion and form it into a disc with a well in the center. Scoop one-quarter of the cream cheese mixture into the well and top with the remaining third of the portion of beef. Form into a patty, sealing up the cheese mixture as much as possible. Repeat with the remaining portions.

4. Preheat the grill to medium. Grill the burgers for 6 to 7 minutes per side for medium doneness, or grill longer if you prefer more well-done burgers. Let rest a few minutes before serving.

 MAKE AHEAD! *These burgers can be formed ahead of time and frozen. Just be sure to let them thaw completely before grilling to ensure that they get cooked through. You can also freeze the fully cooked burgers.*

SERVING SUGGESTION: *Serve with your favorite burger toppings, such as tomatoes, avocado, lettuce, and onion rings. Don't forget the Easy Keto Ketchup (page 136) and some Spicy Refrigerator Pickles (page 134).*

NUTRITIONAL INFORMATION   CALORIES: 418 | FAT: 28.4g | PROTEIN: 35.1g | CARBS: 1.8g | FIBER: 0.3g

MEXICAN CAULIFLOWER RICE SKILLET

This easy skillet meal is one of the most popular recipes on my website. It's a family pleaser and comes together so quickly, you won't know what to do with all that extra time.

👥 (30) 🎯 Yield: 6 servings   Prep time: 5 minutes   Cook time: 20 minutes

1 pound ground beef

¼ medium onion, diced

½ red bell pepper, diced

3 tablespoons taco seasoning

1 cup canned diced tomatoes

12 ounces riced cauliflower (about 3 cups), fresh or frozen

½ cup chicken broth

1½ cups shredded cheddar cheese or Mexican blend cheese (about 6 ounces)

1. In a large skillet over medium heat, brown the ground beef until almost cooked through. Add the onion and bell pepper and continue to cook until the beef is no longer pink. Stir in the taco seasoning.

2. Add the tomatoes and riced cauliflower and stir to combine. Stir in the broth and bring to a simmer. Reduce the heat to medium-low and cook until the cauliflower begins to soften, 8 to 10 minutes.

3. Sprinkle the cheese over the beef and cauliflower mixture and cover the skillet. Cook until the cheese is melted, 3 to 4 minutes.

SERVING SUGGESTION: *Serve with your favorite taco toppings, like sour cream, avocado, tomatoes, black olives, and cilantro.*

NUTRITIONAL INFORMATION   CALORIES: 352 | FAT: 21.7g | PROTEIN: 29.1g | CARBS: 7g | FIBER: 2g

INSTANT POT MEATLOAF

The ultimate comfort food! Meatloaf usually takes a long time to cook in the oven, but this pressure cooker version takes just 25 minutes. And it locks in moisture for a truly delicious meal.

OPTION

Yield: 6 servings   Prep time: 15 minutes   Cook time: 25 minutes

1 pound ground beef

1 pound ground pork

⅓ cup (33g) blanched almond flour

¼ onion, minced

1 teaspoon salt

1 teaspoon black pepper

1 teaspoon garlic powder

½ batch Cheater's Keto Ketchup (page 136)

1. In a large bowl, stir together all of the ingredients except the ketchup. Use your hands to mix well.

2. On a large sheet of aluminum foil, shape the meat mixture into a loaf roughly 5 by 7 inches. Spread the ketchup over the top and sides of the loaf. Shape the foil around the loaf so that it comes partway up the sides, with some space between the meatloaf and the foil.

3. Set the trivet in the bottom of the pressure cooker and add 2 cups of water. Set the meatloaf on top of the trivet.

4. Secure the lid of the pressure cooker and set to manual mode for 25 minutes. Use the quick-release vent and let all of the steam escape before removing the lid. Check that the internal temperature of the meatloaf registers at least 155°F on an instant-read thermometer.

5. Let rest for 5 to 10 minutes before slicing and serving.

NUT-FREE OPTION *I find that almond flour gives this meatloaf the best consistency, but you can substitute crushed pork rinds or ground chia seeds if you prefer.*

SLOW COOKER METHOD *Place a rack (or some balled-up foil) in a 5- or 6-quart slow cooker. Place the meatloaf in its foil cradle on the rack. Do not add water to the slow cooker. Cover with the lid and cook on low for 5 to 6 hours.*

MAKE IT EVEN FASTER! *Feel free to use a store-bought sugar-free ketchup.*

NUTRITIONAL INFORMATION   CALORIES: 422 | FAT: 28.3g | PROTEIN: 34.1g | CARBS: 4.5g | FIBER: 1.3g

CLASSIC ROAST BEEF WITH HORSERADISH CREAM

Shout-out to my father-in-law, who taught me this ridiculously easy way of cooking roast beef. After an initial roast at a high temperature, you simply turn off the oven, which results in a mouthwatering and perfectly cooked roast.

Yield: 8 servings   Prep time: 5 minutes   Cook time: 1 hour 35 minutes

ROAST BEEF:

1 tablespoon coarse salt

2 teaspoons cracked black pepper

1 teaspoon garlic powder

½ teaspoon dried thyme leaves

1 (3-pound) rump roast or eye of round roast, room temperature

GRAVY:

Pan drippings (from roast)

1½ cups beef broth

¼ teaspoon xanthan gum (optional)

HORSERADISH CREAM:

½ cup sour cream

3 tablespoons prepared horseradish

2 teaspoons Dijon mustard

TIP: *It's important to have your roast at room temperature before cooking to ensure that it cooks through properly.*

To make the roast beef:

1. Preheat the oven to 450°F. In a small bowl, whisk together the salt, pepper, garlic powder, and thyme.

2. Pat the roast dry with paper towels and season all over with the seasoning mixture. Place the roast on a rack above a large roasting pan and roast for 25 minutes. Turn the oven off and allow to cook for another hour (or 20 minutes per pound of meat). Do not open the oven door at any time during the cooking process.

3. Remove the roast to a platter and tent with foil. Let rest for 15 minutes. Meanwhile, make the gravy and horseradish cream.

To make the gravy:

1. Transfer the accumulated pan juices to a medium saucepan over medium heat. Whisk in the broth and bring to a boil. Simmer for 5 to 10 minutes, until somewhat reduced.

2. For a thicker gravy, sprinkle the surface with xanthan gum and whisk vigorously to combine.

To make the horseradish cream:

Whisk the ingredients together in a medium bowl.

To serve:

1. Using a very sharp knife, slice the roast as thinly as possible. Serve with the gravy and horseradish cream on the side.

2. Store leftovers in the refrigerator for up to 4 days. The sliced roast also makes great lunchmeat.

NUTRITIONAL INFORMATION   CALORIES: 340 | FAT: 22g | PROTEIN: 33.2g | CARBS: 1.8g | FIBER: 0.4g

CINCINNATI CHILI

Cincinnati chili has a very distinct flavor because of the chocolate, allspice, and cloves. It's usually served over spaghetti or hot dogs and topped with shredded cheese and chopped onions, but we enjoy it straight up or over zucchini noodles.

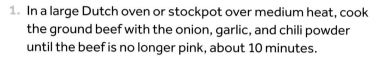 Yield: 8 servings   Prep time: 5 minutes   Cook time: 50 minutes

2 pounds ground beef

½ medium onion, chopped

2 cloves garlic

1 tablespoon chili powder

2 cups Cheater's Tomato Sauce (page 137)

1 cup water

2 tablespoons apple cider vinegar

½ ounce unsweetened chocolate, chopped (optional)

1½ teaspoons salt

1 teaspoon ground cinnamon

½ teaspoon allspice

½ teaspoon cayenne pepper

½ teaspoon ground cloves

½ teaspoon ground cumin

1 bay leaf

1. In a large Dutch oven or stockpot over medium heat, cook the ground beef with the onion, garlic, and chili powder until the beef is no longer pink, about 10 minutes.

2. Stir in the remaining ingredients and bring to a boil. Reduce the heat to low and simmer for 40 minutes. Discard the bay leaf.

3. Store leftovers in the refrigerator for up to 4 days or in the freezer for up to 2 months.

 MAKE AHEAD! *As with so many soups and chilis, Cincinnati chili benefits from being made ahead of time so that the flavors can develop.*

MAKE IT EVEN FASTER! *Use your favorite no-sugar-added tomato sauce in place of the Cheater's Tomato Sauce.*

SERVING SUGGESTION: *When the chili is served over noodles, in this case cooked zucchini noodles, it is called Two-Way Chili. Serving it over noodles and topping it with shredded cheese makes it a Three-Way.*

NUTRITIONAL INFORMATION   CALORIES: 348 | FAT: 21.2g | PROTEIN: 32.3g | CARBS: 7g | FIBER: 2.1g

SLOW COOKER STEAK FAJITAS

Tough cuts like chuck steak benefit from being braised in a slow cooker. This meat becomes so tender, you simply shred it at the end of the cooking time. I like to eat this in a bowl, like soup, but my kids love it with Pork Rind Wraps (page 142).

 Yield: 6 servings Prep time: 5 minutes Cook time: 8 hours

2 pounds chuck steak

3 tablespoons taco seasoning

2 tablespoons avocado oil

2 large bell peppers, any color, thinly sliced

½ medium onion, thinly sliced

¼ cup water

1. Place the chuck steak in a 4- to 6-quart slow cooker and sprinkle with the taco seasoning. Drizzle with the oil and top with the sliced peppers and onions. Pour the water into the slow cooker.

2. Cover and cook on low for 8 hours. Shred the meat with 2 forks before serving.

SERVING SUGGESTION: *Serve with Pork Rind Wraps (page 142) and your favorite fajita toppings, like guacamole, sour cream, shredded cheese, sliced jalapeños, and/or lime wedges.*

NUTRITIONAL INFORMATION CALORIES: 376 | FAT: 29g | PROTEIN: 29.2g | CARBS: 3.6g | FIBER: 1.3g

CHAPTER 4:

PORK

PARMESAN RANCH PORK CHOPS

Ranch seasoning adds a whole new dimension to pan-fried pork chops. Never fear, we aren't using the MSG-laden stuff. A few herbs that you probably already have in your spice drawer will suffice.

Yield: 4 servings   Prep time: 5 minutes   Cook time: 16 minutes

PARMESAN RANCH SEASONING:

¾ ounce Parmesan cheese, grated (about ¾ cup)

1 teaspoon dried dill weed

1 teaspoon garlic powder

½ teaspoon dried parsley

½ teaspoon salt

½ teaspoon black pepper

4 boneless pork chops, about 1 inch thick

Salt and pepper

2 tablespoons avocado oil, for the pan

Chopped fresh parsley, for garnish (optional)

TIP: *If you don't have an ovenproof skillet, you can transfer the seared chops to a rimmed baking sheet or a baking pan.*

1. Preheat the oven to 375°F.

2. In a medium bowl, whisk together the ingredients for the Parmesan ranch seasoning. Set aside.

3. Pat the pork chops dry with paper towels and season both sides with salt and pepper.

4. In a large ovenproof skillet that can hold all of the pork chops, heat the oil over medium-high heat until shimmering. Add the chops and cook for 3 minutes, until nicely browned.

5. Flip the chops over and cook for another 3 minutes. Remove from the heat and sprinkle the top of each chop with the seasoning mixture. Press lightly to adhere.

6. Place the skillet in the oven and cook until the pork reaches an internal temperature of 145°F, 7 to 10 minutes. Serve garnished with fresh parsley, if desired.

NUTRITIONAL INFORMATION   CALORIES: 305 | FAT: 23.3g | PROTEIN: 30.5g | CARBS: 0.9g | FIBER: 0.2g

BACON, MUSHROOM & SWISS FRITTATA

Whenever I am truly stumped for dinner, it's a frittata to the rescue. This flavor combo is perfect for the classic egg dish. You can easily sub in cheddar if you prefer.

30   Yield: 4 servings   Prep time: 10 minutes   Cook time: 20 minutes

6 large eggs

¼ cup heavy cream

8 slices bacon, chopped

4 ounces sliced mushrooms

1 clove garlic, minced

¾ teaspoon salt

½ teaspoon black pepper

1 cup shredded Swiss cheese (about 4 ounces)

1. In a medium bowl, whisk together the eggs and cream until well combined.

2. In a large ovenproof skillet over medium heat, cook the bacon until crisp, about 5 minutes. Remove to a paper towel–lined plate and add the mushrooms to the pan. Sauté for 3 minutes, then add the garlic, salt, and pepper. Continue to cook until the mushrooms are golden brown, about 4 more minutes.

3. Reduce the heat to medium-low and preheat the broiler.

4. Spread the mushrooms evenly across the skillet and sprinkle with the bacon. Pour the egg mixture into the pan and cook until the bottom is set but the top is not quite set, 4 to 6 minutes. Sprinkle with the shredded cheese.

5. Transfer the skillet to the oven, placing it about 5 inches from the heat. Broil until puffy and golden brown, about 2 minutes. Let cool for a few minutes before serving.

NUTRITIONAL INFORMATION   CALORIES: 362 | FAT: 25.3g | PROTEIN: 23.9g | CARBS: 4.4g | FIBER: 0.3g

INSTANT POT CHILE VERDE

Using a multi-cooker such as the wildly popular Instant Pot means that this delicious pork stew is ready in under an hour.

 Yield: 8 servings   Prep time: 15 minutes   Cook time: 45 minutes

2½ pounds boneless pork roast, cut into 1-inch cubes

Salt and pepper

2 tablespoons avocado oil

1 (15-ounce) can salsa verde

1 (4-ounce) can diced green chilies

2 tablespoons chopped pickled jalapeño peppers

2 teaspoons ground cumin

TIP: *Using bottled or canned salsa verde saves tons of time. I purchased the Hatch Chile brand, but La Victoria also has a good one that is low in carbohydrates.*

1. Pat the pork dry with paper towels and season liberally with salt and pepper.

2. Turn the multi-cooker on to the sauté function and add half of the oil. Once it's shimmering, add half of the pork and sauté until nicely browned, 4 to 5 minutes. Transfer to a bowl and repeat with the remaining oil and remaining pork.

3. Return all of the pork to the pot. Add the salsa verde, green chilies, pickled jalapeños, and cumin and stir to combine.

4. Seal the cooker and set on the stew/soup function or on manual high for 35 minutes. When cooking is complete, let the pressure release naturally.

5. Store leftovers in the refrigerator for up to 4 days or in the freezer for up to 2 months.

SLOW COOKER METHOD: *Heat the oil in a large skillet over medium heat. Brown the pork in batches, then transfer to a large slow cooker. Add the remaining ingredients and cook on low for 6 hours.*

SERVING SUGGESTION: *Serve with your favorite toppings, such as sour cream, shredded cheese, lime wedges, diced avocado, and/or chopped cilantro.*

NUTRITIONAL INFORMATION   CALORIES: 425 | FAT: 27.2g | PROTEIN: 35.7g | CARBS: 4.6g | FIBER: 0.6g

SHEET PAN SAUSAGE & PEPPERS

Sheet pan meals are all the rage these days, and for good reason. Throw your meat and veg on a pan, pop the pan in the oven, and you've got dinner.

 👥 (30) 🎯 **Yield:** 6 servings **Prep time:** 5 minutes **Cook time:** 20 minutes

2 medium-sized red bell peppers, thinly sliced

½ medium onion, thinly sliced

2 tablespoons avocado oil

¾ teaspoon salt

½ teaspoon black pepper

½ teaspoon garlic powder

½ teaspoon dried oregano leaves

6 uncooked Italian sausages (about 1½ pounds), spicy or mild

1. Preheat the oven to 425°F.

2. Spread the bell peppers and onion on a rimmed baking sheet. Drizzle with the oil and sprinkle with the salt, pepper, garlic powder, and oregano. Toss to combine and spread out again.

3. Nestle the sausages among the seasoned peppers and onions and bake for 20 minutes.

 MAKE IT EVEN FASTER! *You could use precooked sausages here and save 5 minutes or so of cooking time.*

NUTRITIONAL INFORMATION CALORIES: 377 | FAT: 32.2g | PROTEIN: 16.4g | CARBS: 4.2g | FIBER: 1.1g

ZUCCHINI PAN PIZZA

My kids won't eat zucchini willingly, but they gobbled up this pizza without complaint!

 Yield: 6 servings   Prep time: 10 minutes   Cook time: 30 minutes

ZUCCHINI CRUST:

5 loosely packed cups shredded zucchini (about 1 large zucchini)

1 cup crushed pork rinds

1 cup shredded mozzarella cheese (about 4 ounces)

½ ounce Parmesan cheese, grated (about ½ cup)

1 teaspoon dried oregano leaves

½ teaspoon garlic powder

½ teaspoon salt

½ teaspoon black pepper

1 large egg

TOPPINGS:

½ cup Cheater's Tomato Sauce (page 137)

1 cup shredded mozzarella cheese (about 4 ounces)

3 ounces sliced pepperoni

1. Preheat the oven to 425°F and grease a 13 by 9-inch baking pan.

2. In a large bowl, combine the crust ingredients and mix very well. Press the mixture firmly and evenly into the bottom of the greased baking pan. Bake for 20 minutes, until the crust is firm to the touch and the edges are nicely browned.

3. Spread the crust with the tomato sauce, then sprinkle with the mozzarella and pepperoni. Bake for another 10 minutes, until the cheese is melted and bubbly.

NUTRITIONAL INFORMATION   CALORIES: 291 | FAT: 17.7g | PROTEIN: 21.7g | CARBS: 4.6g | FIBER: 1g

GARLIC ROSEMARY CRUSTED PORK TENDERLOIN

Pork tenderloin doesn't have a lot of fat on it, but it cooks quickly and evenly for an easy weeknight meal.

(30) Yield: 6 servings   Prep time: 5 minutes   Cook time: 25 minutes

¼ cup avocado oil

4 cloves garlic, pressed or minced

3 tablespoons chopped fresh rosemary

2 teaspoons Dijon mustard

1½ teaspoons salt

½ teaspoon black pepper

2 (1-pound) pork tenderloins

1. Preheat the oven to 450°F.

2. In a medium bowl, whisk together the oil, garlic, rosemary, mustard, salt, and pepper.

3. Separate the tenderloins and pat dry with paper towels. Place the tenderloins in a large glass or ceramic baking pan and coat with the garlic-rosemary mixture.

4. Bake for 20 to 25 minutes, until the internal temperature reaches 145°F on an instant-read thermometer. Let rest for a few minutes before slicing.

5. Serve with the pan juices.

SERVING SUGGESTION: *The Cauliflower Rice Pilaf on page 146 rounds out this meal really well.*

NUTRITIONAL INFORMATION   CALORIES: 235 | FAT: 14.5g | PROTEIN: 32.8g | CARBS: 2.4g | FIBER: 0.9g

SMOKED SAUSAGE WITH GARLICKY CAULIFLOWER SPINACH MASH

A keto-friendly version of bangers and mash! Using smoked or precooked sausage cuts down on the cooking time. Just be sure to choose a sausage that has only 1 or 2 grams of carbs per serving.

 (30) Yield: 4 servings   Prep time: 5 minutes, plus time to thaw and drain spinach
Cook time: 20 minutes

1 small head cauliflower, cut into florets

3 cloves garlic

5 ounces frozen spinach, thawed and drained

3 tablespoons salted butter, cut into 3 pieces

Salt and pepper

2 tablespoons avocado oil

1 pound smoked kielbasa or other cooked sausages

½ cup water

1. Place a steamer basket in a large saucepan and fill with a few inches of water. Set over medium heat. Add the cauliflower and garlic cloves and steam until tender, about 7 minutes.

2. Drain the cauliflower and garlic and discard the liquid. Transfer the cauliflower and garlic to a blender or food processor and blend until smooth.

3. Return the blended cauliflower mixture to the empty pot and add the spinach and butter. Set over low heat and cover until the butter is melted. Stir and season to taste with salt and pepper.

4. Meanwhile, heat the oil in a large skillet over medium heat until shimmering. If the smoked sausage you purchased is one long link, cut it into 4 equal portions. Add the sausage and cook until nicely browned on both sides, about 2 minutes per side.

5. Add the water to the pan and cook, covered, until the sausage is heated through, another 5 minutes or so.

6. Divide the cauliflower spinach mash among 4 plates and top with the sausage.

NUTRITIONAL INFORMATION   CALORIES: 419 | FAT: 33.4g | PROTEIN: 11.6g | CARBS: 7.3g | FIBER: 2.2g

ANTIPASTO CAPRESE SALAD

Two of my favorite salads come together in this flavorful dinner salad. It's a great summer meal, and you can easily scale it up or down depending on how many people you plan to serve.

 Yield: 4 servings   Prep time: 10 minutes   Cook time: —

SALAD:

2 ounces sliced pepperoni, cut into strips

2 ounces sliced prosciutto, cut into strips

2 ounces sliced salami, cut into strips

2 ounces sliced provolone cheese, cut into strips

1 cup grape tomatoes, halved

1 cup mini mozzarella balls, halved

½ cup quartered artichoke hearts

½ cup olives

¼ cup chopped pepperoncini

¼ cup chopped fresh basil

DRESSING:

2 tablespoons extra-virgin olive oil

2 tablespoons apple cider vinegar

1 tablespoon balsamic vinegar

2 teaspoons Dijon mustard

1 clove garlic, minced

Salt and pepper

1. In a large bowl, combine all of the salad ingredients.

2. In a small bowl, whisk together the olive oil, apple cider vinegar, balsamic vinegar, mustard, and garlic. Season to taste with salt and pepper.

3. Drizzle the dressing over the salad and toss to combine.

SERVING SUGGESTION: *Make it an even bigger salad by serving it over chopped lettuce.*

NUTRITIONAL INFORMATION   CALORIES: 325 | FAT: 22.2g | PROTEIN: 20.6g | CARBS: 5.3g | FIBER: 1.6g

ZUCCHINI SAUSAGE GRATIN

Every year, our garden overflows with zucchini, and I have to come up with creative ways to serve it to my family. This creamy casserole with sausage is the hit of the summer, by far. It also rewarms really nicely, so you can make it a day or two ahead of serving.

 Yield: 8 servings   **Prep time:** 10 minutes   **Cook time:** 35 minutes

1 pound bulk Italian sausage

2 large zucchini, sliced crosswise into ¼-inch-thick slices

Salt and pepper

2 tablespoons salted butter

2 cloves garlic, minced

1¼ cups heavy whipping cream

¾ ounce Parmesan cheese, grated (about ¾ cup)

¾ cup shredded mozzarella or Italian cheese blend (about 3 ounces)

1. Preheat the oven to 425°F.

2. In a large skillet over medium heat, brown the sausage until cooked through, using a wooden spoon to break up any clumps.

3. In a 13 by 9-inch glass or ceramic baking pan, lay half of the zucchini in an overlapping pattern. Sprinkle with salt and pepper, then top with half of the sausage. Repeat with the remaining zucchini and sausage.

4. In a medium saucepan over medium heat, melt the butter. Add the garlic and sauté until fragrant, about 30 seconds. Stir in the cream and bring just to a simmer. Remove from the heat and stir in the Parmesan until melted.

5. Pour the cream mixture over the zucchini and sausage. Sprinkle with the shredded cheese and bake until bubbly and browned, about 25 minutes.

6. Store leftovers in the refrigerator for up to 4 days.

NUTRITIONAL INFORMATION   CALORIES: 411 | FAT: 35.2g | PROTEIN: 12.8g | CARBS: 6.4g | FIBER: 0.8g

SPICY PORK & CABBAGE STIR-FRY

I love a good stir-fry with a bit of kick to it. Using ground pork makes this recipe come together a little faster.

 (30) Yield: 4 servings   Prep time: 5 minutes   Cook time: 22 minutes

SAUCE:

2 tablespoons soy sauce or coconut aminos

2 tablespoons toasted sesame oil

1 tablespoon Sriracha sauce or other Asian hot sauce

1 clove garlic, minced

½ teaspoon ginger powder

STIR-FRY:

2 tablespoons avocado oil or coconut oil, divided

1 pound ground pork

½ teaspoon salt

½ teaspoon black pepper

½ teaspoon red pepper flakes

4 ounces sliced mushrooms

4 cups shredded cabbage

½ medium-sized red bell pepper, thinly sliced

2 green onions, thinly sliced

2 large eggs, lightly beaten

1. In a small bowl, whisk together the sauce ingredients. Set aside.

2. In a large skillet over medium-high heat, heat 1 tablespoon of the oil. When hot, add the pork and sprinkle with the salt, black pepper, and red pepper flakes. Sauté until the pork is cooked through and no longer pink, 7 to 10 minutes. Transfer to a bowl.

3. Add the remaining 1 tablespoon of oil to the skillet along with the mushrooms and cook until the mushrooms are beginning to brown. Add the cabbage, bell pepper, and green onions and sauté until the cabbage is tender, about 5 minutes.

4. Reduce the heat to medium-low and push the vegetables to the side of the skillet. Pour the beaten eggs into the center and stir to scramble, about 1 minute.

5. Return the pork to the skillet and drizzle with the sauce. Toss to combine and cook for 1 more minute to warm through.

NUTRITIONAL INFORMATION   CALORIES: 443 | FAT: 33.4g | PROTEIN: 23.2g | CARBS: 8.5g | FIBER: 2.6g

SLOW COOKER BBQ PORK RIB BITES

Trader Joe's carries heat-and-eat BBQ Pork Rib Bites, and I always thought they looked delicious. But they are much too carby, so I made my own sugar-free version.

 Yield: 4 servings   Prep time: 10 minutes   Cook time: 6 hours

---

1½ pounds boneless pork ribs (country-style ribs), cut into 1-inch chunks

Salt and pepper

¼ cup tomato paste

2 tablespoons water

2 tablespoons apple cider vinegar

2 tablespoons powdered erythritol

1 teaspoon liquid smoke (optional)

½ teaspoon chipotle powder, or 1 tablespoon chili powder

½ teaspoon garlic powder

⅛ teaspoon cayenne pepper

1. Place the rib bites in a 4- to 6-quart slow cooker and season generously with salt and pepper.

2. In a medium bowl, whisk together the tomato paste, water, vinegar, sweetener, liquid smoke (if using), chipotle powder, garlic powder, and cayenne. Add the sauce to the slow cooker and stir to coat the rib bites. Cover and cook on low for 6 hours.

3. Once cooked, preheat the broiler and line a rimmed baking sheet with foil. Scoop the rib bites out of the sauce and spread them in a single layer on the lined baking sheet. Broil a few inches from the heat for 1 to 2 minutes, until nicely browned. Whisk the sauce that remains in the slow cooker.

4. Serve with the sauce from the slow cooker poured over the rib bites or on the side.

TIP: *You can serve the pork rib bites right out of the slow cooker, but broiling them for a minute or two will give them a more "grilled" appearance and flavor.*

SERVING SUGGESTION: *These rib bites go really well with mashed cauliflower or cauliflower rice.*

NUTRITIONAL INFORMATION   CALORIES: 487 | FAT: 27.7g | PROTEIN: 30.5g | CARBS: 4.5g | FIBER: 1.4g

CHAPTER 5:

L A M B

GYRO LETTUCE WRAPS

My husband is a gyro fanatic, and he used to purchase gyro meat by the case for our freezer. Then we tried making our own version with ground lamb, and we've never looked back.

 Yield: 4 servings   Prep time: 10 minutes   Cook time: 45 minutes

---

TZATZIKI:

½ cup Greek yogurt

½ medium cucumber, quartered lengthwise and thinly sliced crosswise

2 cloves garlic, minced

1 tablespoon chopped fresh dill

1 tablespoon lemon juice

Salt and pepper

GYRO MEAT:

1 pound ground lamb

1½ teaspoons dried ground marjoram

1 teaspoon dried rosemary leaves

1 teaspoon salt

½ teaspoon black pepper

½ teaspoon garlic powder

¼ teaspoon ground cumin

8 large lettuce leaves, for the wraps

1 medium tomato, chopped

¼ cup thinly sliced red onions

1. To make the tzatziki, combine the ingredients in a medium bowl. Set aside.

2. Preheat the oven to 350°F and line a rimmed baking sheet with foil.

3. To make the gyro meat, place the ground lamb and seasonings in a medium bowl and mix well using your hands. Turn the mixture out onto the prepared baking sheet and form into a loaf about 4 by 6 inches. Bake until the internal temperature reaches 160°F, 40 to 45 minutes. Let rest for 10 minutes before slicing thinly.

4. To serve, divide the lettuce leaves among 4 plates. Top with the sliced gyro meat, some chopped tomato, and some sliced onions. Drizzle with the tzatziki or serve the tzatziki on the side.

MAKE AHEAD! *You can make the gyro meat ahead of time. The loaf will keep tightly wrapped in the fridge for up to 3 days or in the freezer for up to a month. Thaw it completely and then slice it thinly. You can pan-fry it to warm it up quickly.*

NUTRITIONAL INFORMATION   CALORIES: 379 | FAT: 23.1g | PROTEIN: 31g | CARBS: 6.4g | FIBER: 1.1g

INDIAN-SPICED LAMB SHANKS & VEGGIES

Lamb shanks are a lot less expensive than other cuts of lamb, but long, slow braising makes them truly tender.

 Yield: 8 servings   Prep time: 10 minutes   Cook time: 2 hours 20 minutes

4 pounds lamb shanks (3 to 4 shanks, depending on size)

1½ tablespoons garam masala

Salt and pepper

4 tablespoons avocado oil, coconut oil, or ghee, divided

2 cups cubed daikon (about 1 medium)

2 cups cubed eggplant (about 1 medium-small)

½ cup chopped onions

1 cup beef broth

1 tablespoon tomato paste

¼ teaspoon red pepper flakes

Chopped fresh cilantro, for garnish (optional)

1. Preheat the oven to 300°F.

2. Pat the lamb shanks dry with paper towels and rub all over with the garam masala. Season generously with salt and pepper.

3. In a large Dutch oven over medium heat, heat 2 tablespoons of the oil until shimmering. Add the lamb shanks and brown on both sides, about 4 minutes per side.

4. Transfer the lamb to a plate and add the remaining 2 tablespoons of oil to the pot. Add the daikon, eggplant, and onions and sauté until the onions are tender, about 5 minutes. Stir in the broth, tomato paste, and red pepper flakes and bring to a simmer.

5. Nestle the lamb shanks into the liquid and vegetables and cover. Transfer the pot to the oven and cook for 2 hours, until the lamb is tender, turning the shanks over once halfway through cooking.

6. Serve garnished with cilantro, if desired. Store leftovers in a covered container in the refrigerator for up to 3 days.

NUTRITIONAL INFORMATION   CALORIES: 431 | FAT: 29.8g | PROTEIN: 38.7g | CARBS: 6.8g | FIBER: 2.8g

MOROCCAN LAMB STEW WITH CAULIFLOWER

The warm spices of cinnamon and cloves make this stew truly comforting. My youngest child loves this recipe and asks me to make it frequently.

Yield: 4 servings   Prep time: 5 minutes   Cook time: 1 hour 30 minutes

MOROCCAN SPICE BLEND:

½ teaspoon ground cinnamon

½ teaspoon ground coriander

½ teaspoon ground cumin

½ teaspoon black pepper

¼ teaspoon cayenne pepper

⅛ teaspoon ground cloves

1½ pounds lamb stew meat

Salt and pepper

¼ cup coconut oil

¼ cup chopped onions

1 clove garlic, minced

1 cup diced tomatoes

1 cup chicken broth

½ medium head cauliflower, cut into florets

1. Preheat the oven to 300°F.

2. To make the spice blend, combine the cinnamon, coriander, cumin, black pepper, cayenne, and cloves in a small bowl. Set aside.

3. Pat the lamb dry with paper towels and season with salt and pepper.

4. In a large Dutch oven over medium heat, heat the oil until shimmering. Place the lamb in the pot and brown on all sides, about 8 minutes. Transfer to a plate using a slotted spoon.

5. Add the onions to the pot and sprinkle with salt. Sauté until translucent, 4 to 5 minutes. Stir in the garlic and the spice mixture and cook until fragrant, about 1 minute. Add the tomatoes and broth and return the lamb to the pot.

6. Bring to a simmer, then cover and transfer the pot to the oven. Cook until the lamb is tender, about 1 hour. Add the cauliflower florets and continue cooking until the cauliflower is tender, another 15 minutes or so.

 MAKE AHEAD! *The warm spices of this stew develop over time, so it's a good one to make a day ahead. It can be refrigerated for up to 4 days. If you plan to freeze it, I would leave out the cauliflower until you warm it up again so the cauliflower doesn't get too soggy.*

NUTRITIONAL INFORMATION   CALORIES: 411 | FAT: 27g | PROTEIN: 32.2g | CARBS: 7.8g | FIBER: 2.4g

BROILED LAMB CHOPS WITH ROSEMARY GARLIC BUTTER

When I was a kid, lamb chops were my favorite food. I would ask for them for my birthday every year. My mum would simply broil them with a little garlic. This is a fresh new take on that recipe, with a delicious rosemary garlic compound butter.

 (30) Yield: 8 chops (2 per serving)   Prep time: 5 minutes, plus 30 minutes to chill butter
Cook time: 10 minutes

¼ cup (½ stick) salted butter, softened

2 cloves garlic, minced

1 tablespoon chopped fresh rosemary

8 lamb loin chops, about 1½ inches thick

Salt and pepper

1. In a medium bowl, combine the butter, garlic, and rosemary. Mash with a fork until well mixed. Place the compound butter on a square of waxed paper and roll into a log. Refrigerate until firm, about 30 minutes.

2. Preheat the broiler. Place the lamb chops on a broiler pan and sprinkle with salt and pepper. Broil about 6 inches from the heat for 5 minutes, then flip over and broil for another 5 minutes or so for medium-rare chops.

3. To serve, top each lamb chop with a pat of the butter.

SERVING SUGGESTION: *Round out your meal with Cheddar Ranch Roasted Cauliflower (page 144) or Cauliflower Rice Pilaf (page 146).*

MAKE IT EVEN FASTER! *If you're in a huge hurry, don't worry about chilling the compound butter completely. It hardly makes a difference in the flavor of the dish.*

NUTRITIONAL INFORMATION   CALORIES: 505 | FAT: 32.2g | PROTEIN: 44.1g | CARBS: 1g | FIBER: 0.4g

CHAPTER 6:

VEGETARIAN

BROCCOLI CHEDDAR QUICHE

Quiche is one of my favorite easy meals. Yes, it takes a little longer to pull together because you have to make the crust, but it's a filling meal that the whole family loves. You can make the crust a day or two ahead and fill it when you're ready. You can also make the whole quiche ahead of time, as it reheats really nicely.

 Yield: 8 servings Prep time: 20 minutes Cook time: 50 minutes

CRUST:

1½ cups (150 g) blanched almond flour

½ teaspoon garlic powder

½ teaspoon salt

¼ cup (½ stick) unsalted butter, melted

FILLING:

8 ounces frozen broccoli, thawed and chopped

4 ounces cheddar cheese, cut into ½-inch cubes

6 large eggs

⅔ cup heavy whipping cream

2 cloves garlic, minced

½ teaspoon salt

½ teaspoon black pepper

¼ cup shredded cheddar cheese (about 1 ounce)

MAKE IT EVEN FASTER! *This quiche is also delicious without the crust. Omitting the crust saves you a step and saves on the carb count, and the quiche tends to cook a little faster, too.*

To make the crust:

1. Preheat the oven to 325°F.

2. In a medium bowl, whisk together the almond flour, garlic powder, and salt. Stir in the melted butter until the dough resembles coarse crumbs.

3. Turn the loose dough out into a 9-inch glass or ceramic pie pan and press firmly into the bottom and up the sides of the pan. Use a flat-bottomed glass or measuring cup to even out the bottom of the crust. Crimp the edges and prick the bottom all over with a fork.

4. Bake the crust for 10 to 12 minutes, until slightly puffed and just starting to brown. Let cool while you prepare the filling.

To make the filling and bake the quiche:

1. Scatter the chopped broccoli and cubed cheese over the crust.

2. In a large bowl, whisk together the eggs, cream, minced garlic, salt, and pepper. Pour over the broccoli and cheese in the crust.

3. Sprinkle with the shredded cheese and bake for 35 to 40 minutes, until the filling is just set in the center. Let cool for 15 minutes before serving.

4. Store in the refrigerator for up to 5 days. Reheat gently in a preheated 300°F oven.

WITH CRUST
NUTRITIONAL INFORMATION CALORIES: 376 | FAT: 31.3g | PROTEIN: 14.8g | CARBS: 7.9g | FIBER: 3.1g

WITHOUT CRUST (SERVES 6)
NUTRITIONAL INFORMATION CALORIES: 272 | FAT: 20.6g | PROTEIN: 13.7g | CARBS: 4.4g | FIBER: 1.1g

GRILLED HALLOUMI EGGPLANT BURGERS

I love using grilled eggplant in place of bread in all sorts of recipes. And a slice of grilled halloumi makes a delicious replacement for a beef burger. This is a light and fresh summer vegetarian meal. You can even top it with more cheese, like sliced cheddar, for a serious cheeseburger!

 Yield: 4 burgers   Prep time: 10 minutes   Cook time: 10 minutes

1 medium eggplant (about 1 pound)

8 ounces halloumi cheese

Salt and pepper

Burger toppings of choice, for serving

1. Preheat the grill to medium.

2. Cut the eggplant crosswise into 8 even slices, about ⅓ inch thick. You may not need the whole eggplant for this recipe. Cut the halloumi into 4 even slices.

3. Place the eggplant and halloumi slices on the preheated grill. Grill the eggplant until tender and slightly charred, about 5 minutes per side. Grill the halloumi until nicely browned, about 3 minutes per side. Watch the cheese carefully to make sure it doesn't get too melted and fall through the grates.

4. Sprinkle the grilled eggplant with salt and pepper. Serve each slice of halloumi between 2 slices of eggplant and top with your favorite burger toppings.

SERVING SUGGESTION: *Try these burgers with Cheater's Keto Ketchup (page 136) and Spicy Refrigerator Pickles (page 134).*

NUTRITIONAL INFORMATION   CALORIES: 255 | FAT: 17.6g | PROTEIN: 15g | CARBS: 8.3g | FIBER: 4.6g

ROASTED TOMATO JALAPEÑO CHEDDAR SOUP

This is creamy, dreamy stuff! It also has a nice little kick to it. It keeps well in the refrigerator for up to a week or can be frozen for up to two months.

Yield: 6 servings   Prep time: 10 minutes   Cook time: 45 minutes

2 pounds fresh tomatoes, coarsely chopped

2 jalapeño peppers, cut in half

2 cloves garlic

¼ cup avocado oil

Salt and pepper

4 cups vegetable broth

4 ounces cream cheese (½ cup)

2 cups shredded cheddar cheese (about 8 ounces)

1. Preheat the oven to 400°F.

2. Spread the tomatoes, jalapeños, and garlic cloves in a single layer in a 13 by 9-inch glass or ceramic baking pan. Drizzle with the oil and season with salt and pepper. Toss well to combine.

3. Roast for 30 minutes, until the tomatoes have begun to caramelize. Transfer to a large saucepan set over medium heat. Add the broth and bring to a simmer.

4. Add the cream cheese and stir until melted. Use an immersion blender to puree the soup until smooth. Alternatively, you can puree the soup in batches in a blender or food processor and then return it to the pot.

5. Add the shredded cheddar and stir until melted.

SERVING SUGGESTION: *Garnish with sliced jalapeños and extra shredded cheese. If you don't need the soup to be vegetarian, try adding some crumbled cooked sausage. It's amazing!*

NUTRITIONAL INFORMATION   CALORIES: 292 | FAT: 26.1g | PROTEIN: 11.3g | CARBS: 8.3g | FIBER: 1.5g

SPINACH & ARTICHOKE-STUFFED PORTOBELLOS

(30) Yield: 4 mushroom caps (1 per serving)   Prep time: 10 minutes   Cook time: 17 minutes

4 portobello mushroom caps

2 tablespoons avocado oil

Salt and pepper

STUFFING:

4 ounces frozen artichoke hearts, thawed and chopped

4 ounces frozen spinach, thawed, drained, and squeezed of excess liquid

½ cup mayonnaise

1 ounce Parmesan cheese, grated (about 1 cup)

2 cloves garlic, minced

¾ teaspoon salt

½ teaspoon black pepper

2 large eggs

1 cup shredded mozzarella cheese (about 4 ounces)

1. Preheat the oven to 400°F and line a rimmed baking sheet with foil or parchment paper.

2. Remove the stems and gills from the mushroom caps and brush the insides and outsides with the oil. Season the insides of the caps with salt and pepper. Place in a glass or ceramic baking pan that is large enough to fit all of the mushroom caps in a single layer.

3. To make the stuffing, stir together the artichoke hearts, spinach, mayonnaise, Parmesan, garlic, salt, and pepper in a medium bowl. Add the eggs and stir until well combined.

4. Divide the stuffing mixture among the prepared mushroom caps, pressing it into the caps to fill.

5. Sprinkle each stuffed mushroom with ¼ cup of the shredded mozzarella. Bake for 15 minutes, until the cheese is melted and the mushrooms are tender. Turn on the broiler and broil the caps for a minute or two, until the cheese is lightly browned.

NUTRITIONAL INFORMATION   CALORIES: 380 | FAT: 28.5g | PROTEIN: 20.1g | CARBS: 8.2g | FIBER: 2.7g

ZUCCHINI PIE

When my husband and I were first married, someone gave us a recipe for a zucchini pie made with Bisquick. It suited our taste buds and our limited newlywed budget. This is my updated keto take on that old favorite; the addition of crumbled feta was my husband's inspiration. This dish reheats well, so it can easily be made a day or two ahead.

OPTION

 Yield: 6 servings   Prep time: 10 minutes   Cook time: 35 to 40 minutes

---

7 large eggs

⅓ cup avocado oil

2 cloves garlic, minced

¾ teaspoon salt

½ teaspoon black pepper

½ teaspoon dried marjoram leaves

⅓ cup coconut flour

1½ teaspoons baking powder

1 medium zucchini, sliced crosswise in ¼-inch-thick rounds

½ ounce Parmesan cheese, grated (about ½ cup)

½ cup crumbled feta cheese (about 2 ounces)

1. Preheat the oven to 375°F and grease a 9-inch glass or ceramic pie pan.

2. In a large bowl, whisk together the eggs, oil, garlic, salt, pepper, and marjoram. Whisk in the coconut flour and baking powder until well combined.

3. Add the zucchini, Parmesan, and feta and stir to mix well. Spread in the greased pie pan and bake for 35 to 40 minutes, until the top is puffed and golden brown. Remove from the oven and let cool for 10 minutes before slicing.

4. Reheat leftover pie in a preheated 300°F oven. It can also be microwaved on high, but it heats up quickly, so check it often.

DAIRY-FREE OPTION: *Leave out the cheeses if you want a dairy-free version. You can add a few tablespoons of nutritional yeast to give the pie a cheesy flavor.*

NUTRITIONAL INFORMATION   CALORIES: 279 | FAT: 30.3g | PROTEIN: 13.1g | CARBS: 6.7g | FIBER: 2.6g

CHAPTER 7:

EXTRAS

SPICY REFRIGERATOR PICKLES

We are a family of pickle lovers, and we pair them with almost everything. We also just stand over the jar and spoon them straight into our mouths. These easy refrigerator pickles don't require the intense labor of canning, and they have a wonderful fresh crispness. I make a huge batch every summer, and we enjoy them for months.

 Yield: 3 pints (about thirty 1-ounce servings)   Prep time: 15 minutes
Cook time: 5 minutes

2 pounds pickling cucumbers, sliced into ¼-inch-thick rounds

1 jalapeño pepper, cut lengthwise into 6 strips

2 cloves garlic, coarsely chopped

2 tablespoons chopped fresh dill

1½ teaspoons whole black peppercorns

1½ teaspoons ground coriander

1½ cups white vinegar

¾ cup apple cider vinegar

¾ cup water

¼ cup coarse salt

1. Divide the cucumber slices, jalapeño strips, garlic, dill, peppercorns, and coriander evenly among 3 pint jars.

2. In a large saucepan, combine the white vinegar, apple cider vinegar, water, and salt. Bring to a boil, stirring to dissolve most of the salt. Divide the brine among the jars, filling them to about 1 inch from the top. If you don't have quite enough brine to fill the jars to the top, simply add a little more water. Screw the lids on the jars.

3. Leave the jars on the counter for 3 days, then transfer to the refrigerator. The pickles can be eaten at this point but are best after 2 to 3 weeks, when the flavors have had time to fully develop.

4. Store in the refrigerator for up to 3 months.

NUTRITIONAL INFORMATION   CALORIES: 4 | FAT: 0g | PROTEIN: 0.2g | CARBS: 1.2g | FIBER: 0.2g

CHEATER'S KETO KETCHUP

You could spend all your time boiling tomatoes down to a thick ketchup, or you could whisk together some tomato paste, water, and a few spices and call it done. The latter is much more my style!

 (30) Yield: about ½ cup (8 servings) Prep time: 2 minutes Cook time: —

½ cup tomato paste

3 tablespoons water

1 tablespoon apple cider vinegar

1 tablespoon powdered erythritol

½ teaspoon Worcestershire sauce

¼ teaspoon salt

⅛ teaspoon garlic powder

Pinch of ground allspice

Whisk all of the ingredients together until smooth. Store in the refrigerator for up to a week.

NUTRITIONAL INFORMATION CALORIES: 7 | FAT: 0g | PROTEIN: 0.4g | CARBS: 1.7g | FIBER: 0.3g

CHEATER'S TOMATO SAUCE

While no-sugar-added tomato sauce is completely acceptable for the easy dinner recipes in this book, I don't always have some on hand. So I whip up this cheater's version for recipes like Chicken Parmesan Casserole (page 42).

30 Yield: 1 cup (4 servings)   Prep time: 2 minutes   Cook time: —

¼ cup tomato paste

¾ cup hot water

¾ teaspoon garlic powder

½ teaspoon dried oregano leaves

Salt and pepper, to taste

Whisk all of the ingredients together until smooth. Store in the refrigerator for up to a week.

COCONUT FLOUR 90-SECOND BREAD

Nothing, and I mean nothing, is faster than this easy keto bread recipe. You can whip it up any old time you feel like it, and you can make several breads at once. It's particularly delicious toasted.

OPTION

 (30) Yield: 1 bread round   Prep time: 2 minutes   Cook time: 90 seconds

---

2 tablespoons salted butter, melted

1½ tablespoons coconut flour

½ teaspoon baking powder

Pinch of salt

1 large egg

1. Grease an 8-ounce ramekin well.

2. In a small bowl, whisk together the melted butter, coconut flour, baking powder, and salt. Add the egg and whisk until well combined.

3. Spread the batter in the greased ramekin and microwave on high for 90 seconds. Let cool for a few minutes before flipping out of the ramekin.

4. Slice in half to toast.

TIP: *This bread tends to be very moist when it first comes out of the ramekin. I like to make it about an hour ahead and let it dry out on a cooling rack so it has a more bready consistency. It's pretty hefty on its own, coming in at a whopping 320 calories and 27 grams of fat. It's filling stuff, so I typically eat only half at a time. It's perfect for Classic Tuna Melts (page 54).*

DAIRY-FREE OPTION: *Use avocado oil or melted coconut oil in place of the butter if you need the bread to be dairy-free.*

NUTRITIONAL INFORMATION   CALORIES: 320 | FAT: 27.3g | PROTEIN: 8g | CARBS: 7g | FIBER: 3.8g

CHEESY DROP BISCUITS

These easy low-carb biscuits are perfect with everything from Cincinnati Chili (page 82) to Roasted Tomato Jalapeño Cheddar Soup (page 126).

  Yield: 12 biscuits   Prep time: 10 minutes   Cook time: 25 minutes

½ cup (50g) blanched almond flour

½ cup (55g) coconut flour

2 teaspoons baking powder

1 teaspoon garlic powder

½ teaspoon salt

¾ cup shredded cheddar cheese (about 3 ounces), divided

3 large egg whites

2 large whole eggs

¾ cup sour cream or plain Greek yogurt

¼ cup (½ stick) unsalted butter, melted

1. Preheat the oven to 350°F and line a baking sheet with parchment paper or a silicone baking mat.

2. In a large bowl, whisk together the almond flour, coconut flour, baking powder, garlic powder, and salt. Whisk in ½ cup of the shredded cheese. Stir in the egg whites, whole eggs, sour cream, and melted butter until well combined.

3. Drop the dough by rounded spoonfuls onto the lined baking sheet, leaving an inch or two of space between them, as the biscuits will spread as they cook. Sprinkle the tops with the remaining ¼ cup of shredded cheese.

4. Bake for 20 to 25 minutes, until golden brown and firm to the touch. Let cool on the baking sheet for 10 minutes before serving.

TIP: *If you don't want to have leftover egg yolks, you can use 4 whole eggs in place of the 3 egg whites and 2 whole eggs. But I think these biscuits have a better consistency and lightness when made with the egg whites.*

MAKE AHEAD! *These biscuits will keep in the refrigerator for up to a week, and they rewarm really well in a preheated 300°F oven.*

NUTRITIONAL INFORMATION CALORIES: 154 | FAT: 11.9g | PROTEIN: 5.7g | CARBS: 4.7g | FIBER: 2.2g

PORK RIND WRAPS

The idea of using crushed pork rinds for tortillas and wraps is nothing new, but most recipes use cream cheese as a binder. I was determined to make a dairy-free version that would still hold up to delicious fillings. It took a number of tries to get the proportions right. I discovered that the collagen in the pork skin helps bind the ingredients without the addition of cream cheese. These are like thin savory crepes and are great for wrapping up Slow Cooker Steak Fajitas (page 84) or sopping up the juices from Instant Pot Chile Verde (page 92). I also like them filled with tuna salad.

Yield: 8 wraps   Prep time: 10 minutes   Cook time: 30 minutes

4 large eggs

3 ounces pork rinds, crushed

½ teaspoon garlic powder

¼ teaspoon ground cumin

¼ to ½ cup water

Avocado oil or coconut oil, for the pan

1. In a high-powered blender or food processor, combine the eggs, pork rinds, garlic powder, and cumin. Blend until smooth and well combined. Add ¼ cup of the water and blend again. If the mixture is very thick, continue to add water until it is the consistency of pancake batter.

2. Heat a scant ½ teaspoon of oil in an 8-inch nonstick skillet over medium-low heat. Swirl to coat the pan. Add about 3 tablespoons of the batter and use a rubber spatula to spread it thinly over the bottom of the pan, almost to the edges.

3. Cook for about a minute, until the bottom is beginning to brown. Loosen the edges and carefully flip. Cook the second side for another minute or so.

4. Repeat with the remaining batter, adding oil to the skillet only as necessary (the batter spreads and cooks better with less oil in the pan).

5. Add more water to the batter as needed; it will thicken as it sits.

MAKE AHEAD! *Because these wraps are cooked one at a time, they are a bit time-consuming, but they keep well in the refrigerator for up to 5 days. Store them in a covered container.*

NUTRITIONAL INFORMATION   CALORIES: 94 | FAT: 5.6g | PROTEIN: 9.7g | CARBS: 0.4g | FIBER: 0g

CHEDDAR RANCH ROASTED CAULIFLOWER

I love roasted cauliflower! And while my children may not love it quite as much as I do, they eat it willingly. This side goes with just about any meat dish in this book.

(30) Yield: 6 servings   Prep time: 5 minutes   Cook time: 25 minutes

1 medium head cauliflower, cut into 1-inch florets

2 tablespoons avocado oil

1 teaspoon salt

½ teaspoon black pepper

1 teaspoon dried dill weed

½ teaspoon dried parsley

½ teaspoon garlic powder

½ teaspoon onion powder

1 cup shredded cheddar cheese (about 4 ounces)

1. Preheat the oven to 400°F.

2. Spread the cauliflower on a large rimmed baking sheet and drizzle with the oil. Sprinkle with the salt and pepper and toss to coat. Spread back out in a single layer and roast for 20 minutes, or until tender and beginning to brown.

3. Meanwhile, combine the dill, parsley, garlic powder, and onion powder in a small bowl.

4. Remove the cauliflower from the oven and sprinkle with the seasonings and shredded cheese. Toss again to coat, then return to the oven for 5 minutes to melt the cheese.

NUTRITIONAL INFORMATION   CALORIES: 134 | FAT: 12.7g | PROTEIN: 6.5g | CARBS: 5.4g | FIBER: 2g

CAULIFLOWER RICE PILAF WITH BASIL & PINE NUTS

It turns out that rice pilaf is just as good when it's made with cauliflower rice. This is a perfect side dish for Butter-Roasted Salmon (page 50) or Garlic Parmesan Crusted Pork Tenderloin (page 98). It would also be great with Broiled Lamb Chops (page 118).

OPTION

(30)   Yield: 6 servings   Prep time: 10 minutes   Cook time: 15 minutes

¼ cup (½ stick) salted butter

¼ cup finely chopped onions

½ teaspoon salt

½ teaspoon black pepper

4 cups riced cauliflower

2 tablespoons chicken broth or water

2 tablespoons toasted pine nuts

1 tablespoon finely chopped fresh basil

1. In a large skillet over medium heat, melt the butter. Add the onions and sprinkle with the salt and pepper. Sauté until the onions are tender, about 3 minutes.

2. Add the riced cauliflower and toss to coat in the butter. Cook for 5 minutes, stirring frequently.

3. Add the broth and cover. Cook until tender, another 4 to 5 minutes. Stir in the pine nuts and chopped basil.

 **DAIRY-FREE OPTION:** *Replace the butter with avocado oil.*

NUTRITIONAL INFORMATION   CALORIES: 114 | FAT: 9g | PROTEIN: 2.5g | CARBS: 6g | FIBER: 2.2g

CARAMELIZED BRUSSELS SPROUTS WITH BROWNED BUTTER

This is the recipe that finally got my husband to accept Brussels sprouts into his life. If that's not a ringing endorsement, I don't know what is!

(30) Yield: 4 servings   Prep time: 5 minutes   Cook time: 10 minutes

1 tablespoon coconut oil or avocado oil

¾ pound Brussels sprouts, trimmed and halved

¾ teaspoon salt

½ teaspoon black pepper

3 tablespoons salted butter

1. Heat the oil in a large skillet over medium-high heat until shimmering but not smoking.

2. Lay the Brussels sprouts cut side down in a single layer in the skillet and cook until nicely browned, 2 to 3 minutes. Toss quickly with a spatula, cover the pan, and cook for another 2 minutes, until the sprouts are just becoming tender. Transfer the sprouts to a medium bowl and sprinkle with the salt and pepper.

3. Add the butter to the hot skillet, reduce the heat to medium, and cook until browned and fragrant, 3 to 4 minutes.

4. Drizzle the butter over the sprouts and serve immediately. Season with more salt and pepper to taste.

NUTRITIONAL INFORMATION   CALORIES: 143 | FAT: 11.7g | PROTEIN: 3g | CARBS: 7.8g | FIBER: 3.3g

SLOW COOKER THREE-CHEESE SPAGHETTI SQUASH

Realizing that I could cook spaghetti squash in my slow cooker was an absolute revelation. This easy recipe has you mixing the rest of the ingredients right in the slow cooker as well, so there are no other pots, pans, or bowls to wash!

 Yield: 6 servings   **Prep time:** 15 minutes   **Cook time:** 3 hours 10 minutes

1 large spaghetti squash

¼ cup (½ stick) salted butter

2 cloves garlic, minced

1½ ounces Asiago cheese, grated (about 1½ cups)

1½ ounces Parmesan cheese, grated (about 1½ cups)

¾ teaspoon salt

½ teaspoon black pepper

¾ cup shredded mozzarella cheese (about 3 ounces)

¼ cup chopped fresh basil

1. Cut the spaghetti squash in half crosswise. Place the halves cut side down in a 4- to 6-quart slow cooker and cook on high for 2 to 3 hours or on low for 4 to 6 hours. The squash is cooked when it can easily be squeezed.

2. Turn off the slow cooker and remove the squash. Add the butter and garlic to the slow cooker and let the butter melt.

3. Meanwhile, use a large spoon to scoop the seeds out of the spaghetti squash. Discard the seeds. Scoop the flesh out of the skin and return it to the slow cooker. Add the Asiago, Parmesan, salt, and pepper and toss to combine the ingredients. Spread evenly in the bottom of the slow cooker.

4. Sprinkle with the mozzarella and replace the slow cooker lid. Let sit in the warm slow cooker until the cheese is melted, another 10 minutes or so. Sprinkle with fresh basil and serve.

NUTRITIONAL INFORMATION   CALORIES: 144 | FAT: 10.5g | PROTEIN: 6.2g | CARBS: 6g | FIBER: 1.2g

ACKNOWLEDGMENTS

Tim, Austin, Celia, and Maggie—My loving family and my recipe testers extraordinaire! Thanks for lending me your taste buds for this project. I know I will always get your most honest opinions. I couldn't do this without your love and support.

Victory Belt—The best publishing company in the world. Erich, thanks for your faith in me and for handing me more projects. Susan, I love our chats and your encouragement. Holly, your advice is invaluable in getting these recipes into tiptop shape. Lance, Pam, and the whole VB team, you put together the best keto books on the market. But you already knew that . . .

Bill and Hayley—Thanks for bringing my cover image ideas to life.

Readers and fans—Without you and your encouragement, there would be no cookbooks. I sincerely hope that you love the recipes on these pages and that they help you get healthy dinners on the table every night. *Bon appétit!*

RECOMMENDED CONVENIENCE FOODS

I get it. Time is of the essence, and it's perfectly acceptable to rely on some store-bought items to help simplify your dinner prep. The keto police will not come and arrest you for it, I promise. These prepared products can make getting keto dinners on the table even easier. All of them are high-quality and keto-friendly low-carb foods.

Broth

- **Epic**—Pricey and made from grass-fed and pastured animals.

- **Kettle & Fire**—Pricey but delicious! Made from grass-fed and pastured animals.

- **O Organics**—The signature brand carried by Albertsons, Safeway, and other stores under the Albertsons umbrella. It's a great value.

- **Pacific Foods**—This brand is probably the easiest to find, as most grocery stores have it in stock.

- **Zoup!**—Not organic but a little more budget-friendly.

Tomato Sauce

Store-bought tomato sauce can contain a shocking amount of carbohydrates, even if there is no added sugar. Some products have 10 or more grams per ½-cup serving, while others, like those listed below, have 5 grams or less. The moral of the story is to read your labels!

- **Mezzetta**—Only 5 grams per ½ cup.

- **Organico Bello**—The marinara and tomato basil sauces have only 4 grams of carbs per ½ cup.

- **Rao's Homemade**—The marinara sauce is the lowest-carb option at 4 grams per ½ cup.

Ketchup

- **AlternaSweets**—Sweetened with stevia.
- **Elevation Organic**—Made with coconut nectar but still very low in carbs.
- **Health Garden**—Sweetened with xylitol.
- **Low Carb Foods**—Sweetened with stevia and erythritol.
- **Nature's Hollow**—Sweetened with xylitol.

Mayonnaise

- **Chosen Foods Coconut Oil Mayo**—Comes in traditional flavor and a variety of other flavors. Traditional has the fewest carbs.
- **Chosen Foods Mayo**—Made with avocado oil, and a little less expensive than Primal Kitchen brand. Sometimes you can find it at Costco.
- **Coconaise**—Made with coconut oil and MCT oil.
- **Primal Kitchen**—Made with avocado oil.

Taco Seasoning and Other Seasoning Blends

- **Penzey's**—This famous purveyor is well known for the high quality of its spices and blends. I love the Tandoori, Garam Masala, and Hot Curry blends, which are all just spices with no additives. They do add some flours and sugar to a few of their blends, so be a label reader.
- **Primal Palate**—From the wonderful people behind the Primal Palate website—who also happened to be the cover photographers for this book!
- **Spice Cave/Spiceologist**—This brand is from a blogger friend of mine and has gained considerable popularity. The company is very careful to avoid the additives and sprays used on many commercial herbs and spices.

Salsa

Most brands of traditional tomato salsa contain only about 2 grams of carbs per serving. Steer clear of salsas that contain fruit or beans, as those tend to be higher in carbs. Salsa verde (tomatillo salsa) also tends to be quite low in carbs. The following are a few brands I like:

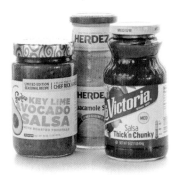

- Frontera
- Hatch
- La Victoria
- O Organics

Sausage (Fully Cooked)

- **Aidells Chicken Sausage**—Andouille and Habanero with Pepper Jack are the two varieties with only 1 gram of carbs per serving.
- **Al Fresco Gourmet**—The Red Pepper & Asiago, Buffalo Chicken, and Spinach & Feta varieties all have only 1 gram of carbs per serving.
- **Kiolbassa Smoked Meats**—My husband buys this organic Polish-style sausage at Costco, and it's delicious. It's worth finding a place near you that carries it!

- **Teton Waters Ranch**—All varieties of these grass-fed beef dinner sausages are fully cooked and have only 1 gram of carbs. We love the Cheddar Jalapeño Brats and the smoked Polish sausage. The hot dogs are fabulous, too.

Riced Cauliflower

- **Bird's Eye**—Available in many stores with some fun flavors.
- **Boulder Canyon**—I haven't tried this one, but they also carry riced broccoli.
- **Green Giant**—Also widely available. Be sure to stick with the plain variety, as some of the Vegetable Medleys have more carbs.
- **Trader Joe's Organic Frozen**—This is my favorite because it has such perfectly even grains of cauliflower rice.

RECIPE INDEX

CHAPTER 1: CHICKEN

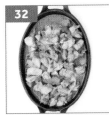

CHAPTER 2: FISH AND SEAFOOD

48
Greek Shrimp

50
Butter-Roasted Salmon with Lemony Dill Aioli

52
California Roll in a Bowl

54
Classic Tuna Melts

56
Smoked Salmon Chowder

58
Creamy Pesto Shrimp & Zoodles

60
Blackened Shrimp Spinach Salad

CHAPTER 3: BEEF

64
French Onion Pot Roast

66
Bacon Sloppy Joes

68
Reuben Skillet

70
Beef & Mushroom Stew

72
Grilled Flank Steak with Cowboy Butter

74
Jalapeño Cheddar Stuffed Burgers

76
Mexican Cauliflower Rice Skillet

78
Instant Pot Meatloaf

80
Classic Roast Beef with Horseradish Cream

82
Cincinnati Chili

Slow Cooker
Steak Fajitas

CHAPTER 4: PORK

Parmesan Ranch
Pork Chops

Bacon, Mushroom &
Swiss Frittata

Instant Pot Chile Verde

Sheet Pan
Sausage & Peppers

Zucchini Pan Pizza

Garlic Rosemary
Crusted
Pork Tenderloin

Smoked Sausage with
Garlicky Cauliflower
Spinach Mash

Antipasto
Caprese Salad

Zucchini Sausage
Gratin

Spicy Pork & Cabbage
Stir-Fry

Slow Cooker
BBQ Pork Rib Bites

CHAPTER 5: LAMB

112

Gyro Lettuce Wraps

114

Indian-Spiced
Lamb Shanks &
Veggies

116

Moroccan Lamb Stew
with Cauliflower

118

Broiled Lamb Chops
with Rosemary
Garlic Butter

CHAPTER 6: VEGETARIAN

122

Broccoli Cheddar
Quiche

124

Grilled Halloumi
Eggplant Burgers

126

Roasted Tomato
Jalapeño Cheddar
Soup

128

Spinach & Artichoke–
Stuffed Portobellos

130

Zucchini Pie

CHAPTER 7: EXTRAS

134
Spicy Refrigerator Pickles

136
Cheater's Keto Ketchup

137
Cheater's Tomato Sauce

138
Coconut Flour 90-Second Bread

140
Cheesy Drop Biscuits

142
Pork Rind Wraps

144
Cheddar Ranch Roasted Cauliflower

146
Cauliflower Rice Pilaf with Basil & Pine Nuts

148
Caramelized Brussels Sprouts with Browned Butter

150
Slow Cooker Three-Cheese Spaghetti Squash

RECIPE QUICK REFERENCE

O = option

RECIPES	PAGE	🍳	⊙	🔪	👥	❄	▭	30	◎	🏠
Chicken Enchilada Skillet	22				✓			✓	✓	
Cilantro Lime Grilled Chicken	24	✓			✓	✓	✓	✓		
Italian Chicken & Veggie Foil Packets	26	O								
One-Pan Jamaican Jerk Chicken & "Rice"	28	✓			✓				✓	
Southwestern Chicken–Stuffed Avocados	30	O						✓		
Chicken Coconut Curry	32	✓							✓	
Buffalo Chicken Chowder	34				✓			✓		
Bacon Spinach Feta Chicken	36				✓			✓	✓	
Slow Cooker White Chicken Chili	38	✓			✓	✓				✓
Thai Chicken Salad	40	✓						✓		
Chicken Parmesan Casserole	42				✓	✓	✓	✓		
Spicy Tandoori Chicken	44				✓	✓	✓			
Greek Shrimp	48							✓	✓	
Butter-Roasted Salmon with Lemony Dill Aioli	50	O			✓			✓	✓	
California Roll in a Bowl	52	O						✓		
Classic Tuna Melts	54				✓			✓		
Smoked Salmon Chowder	56							✓		
Creamy Pesto Shrimp & Zoodles	58							✓	✓	
Blackened Shrimp Spinach Salad	60							✓		
French Onion Pot Roast	64	✓			✓					✓
Bacon Sloppy Joes	66	✓			✓	✓		✓	✓	
Reuben Skillet	68				✓			✓	✓	
Beef & Mushroom Stew	70	✓					✓		✓	✓
Grilled Flank Steak with Cowboy Butter	72				✓			✓		
Jalapeño Cheddar Stuffed Burgers	74				✓	✓	✓			
Mexican Cauliflower Rice Skillet	76				✓			✓	✓	
Instant Pot Meatloaf	78			O	✓	✓				
Classic Roast Beef with Horseradish Cream	80				✓					✓
Cincinnati Chili	82	✓			✓	✓	✓		✓	
Slow Cooker Steak Fajitas	84	✓							✓	✓

RECIPES	PAGE							30		
Parmesan Ranch Pork Chops	88				✓			✓	✓	
Bacon, Mushroom & Swiss Frittata	90		✓					✓	✓	
Instant Pot Chile Verde	92	✓			✓	✓				
Sheet Pan Sausage & Peppers	94	✓			✓			✓	✓	
Zucchini Pan Pizza	96		✓		✓					
Garlic Rosemary Crusted Pork Tenderloin	98	✓			✓			✓		
Smoked Sausage	100				✓			✓		
Antipasto Caprese Salad	102							✓		
Zucchini Sausage Gratin	104				✓		✓			
Spicy Pork & Cabbage Stir-Fry	106	✓	✓					✓	✓	
Slow Cooker BBQ Pork Rib Bites	108	✓			✓					✓
Gyro Lettuce Wraps	112				✓		✓			
Indian-Spiced Lamb Shanks & Veggies	114	✓			✓					✓
Moroccan Lamb Stew with Cauliflower	116	✓			✓		✓		✓	✓
Broiled Lamb Chops with Rosemary Garlic Butter	118				✓			✓		
Broccoli Cheddar Quiche	122		✓	✓	✓		✓			
Grilled Halloumi Eggplant Burgers	124							✓		
Roasted Tomato Jalapeño Cheddar Soup	126					✓	✓			
Spinach & Artichoke–Stuffed Portobellos	128		✓					✓	✓	
Zucchini Pie	130	O	✓		✓		✓			
Spicy Refrigerator Pickles	134	✓			✓					
Cheater's Keto Ketchup	136	✓			✓			✓		
Cheater's Tomato Sauce	137	✓						✓		
Coconut Flour 90-Second Bread	138	O	✓		✓			✓		
Cheesy Drop Biscuits	140		✓	✓	✓		✓			
Pork Rind Wraps	142	✓	✓		✓		✓			
Cheddar Ranch Roasted Cauliflower	144				✓			✓	✓	
Cauliflower Rice Pilaf	146	O		✓				✓	✓	
Caramelized Brussels Sprouts	148							✓	✓	
Slow Cooker Three-Cheese Spaghetti Squash	150				✓				✓	✓

GENERAL INDEX

ABOUT THE AUTHOR

Carolyn Ketchum is the writer, photographer, and evil mastermind behind *All Day I Dream About Food,* a low-carb, gluten-free food blog, and the author of *Everyday Ketogenic Kitchen. ADIDAF* is one of the most popular low-carb sites on the internet and has a devoted following among dieters, diabetics, and those simply trying to live a healthier lifestyle. Carolyn's mission is to prove to the world that special diets need not be boring or restrictive. It's astonishing what you can do with a bag of almond flour, a stick of butter, and a willingness to experiment.

The way Carolyn sees it, she didn't choose the low-carb lifestyle; it chose her. After being diagnosed with gestational diabetes during her third pregnancy, she began watching her carb intake. And when the diabetes decided to stick around, she refused to give up her lifelong passion for baking and cooking; she just had to find new ways to do it. To her delight, she discovered that with a little ingenuity and some perseverance, many high-carb recipes can be made over into low-carb treats without sacrificing flavor.

Carolyn has a master's degree in anthropology and early human evolution and an extensive background in higher education administration. She lives in Portland, Oregon, with her husband and three children.